PEOPLES AND CUSTOMS OF THE WORLD

HUNTING, HARVESTING AND HOME

JACQUELINE DINEEN

ILLUSTRATED BY ROBERT INGPEN
Consultant: PHILIP WILKINSON

DRAGON'S WORLD

CHILDREN'S BOOKS

Dragon's World Ltd
Limpsfield
Surrey RH8 0DY
Great Britain

First published by Dragon's World Ltd, 1995

© Dragon's World Ltd, 1995
© Text by Dragon's World Ltd, 1995
© Illustrations by Robert Ingpen, 1994 and 1995

Text and captions by **Jacqueline Dineen**
based on *A Celebration of Customs & Rituals of the World*
by Robert Ingpen and Philip Wilkinson.

Editor: Diana Briscoe
Designer: Megra Mitchell
Art Director: John Strange
Design Assistants: Victoria Furbisher
and Karen Ferguson
Editorial Director: Pippa Rubinstein

British Library Cataloguing in Publication Data
The catalogue record for this book is available from the British Library.

ISBN 1 85028 303 6

Typeset in Bembo, Garamond and
Opti-Announcement by Dragon's World Ltd
Printed in Italy

Contents

Introduction

What do you need to survive? You need a healthy body, you need shelter, and you need food and drink. These are the basic needs of all animals, including people. No matter how important other aspects of life may be, no matter how important and powerful a nation becomes, food remains the most basic need which has to be met. From the earliest times, people have spent much of their lives finding or producing food. The first people who roamed the Earth lived by hunting animals and gathering plants which they could eat. Their whole lives revolved around this search, for they soon learned that if they could not find enough food, they would die.

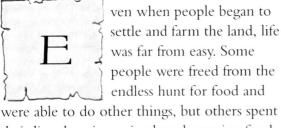

Even when people began to settle and farm the land, life was far from easy. Some people were freed from the endless hunt for food and were able to do other things, but others spent their lives keeping animals and growing food, as farmers still do today. They domesticated certain animals for meat and milk. Crops could be grown to order.

However, now other factors assumed importance. The main one was the weather. Plants would not grow without sunshine and water. Animals could not live without food. They needed grassy fields to graze in or crops grown for them. Even animals which could survive on the sparse vegetation of desert regions needed enough to keep them going. The earliest settlements were near rivers such as the Tigris and Euphrates in Mesopotamia and the Nile in Egypt. Here at least, people could be reasonably sure of getting water for their crops, if they could find ways of channelling it to the fields. But still they relied on the rains to top up the rivers and make them flood over the surrounding land, carrying fertile soil with them.

Farmers learned that the weather could be fickle. The rains expected at a certain time of year might be late or might not come at all. In colder climates, the sun sometimes did not shine enough to make the plants grow. People began to believe that gods were responsible for making the sun shine or the rain fall. At certain times of year, they would pray for rain and sunshine. Many ancient civilizations had gods who were responsible for the sun, the rain, the fertility of the soil, and even the crops themselves. People developed special rituals to ask the gods for rain and sun, and to thank them when the crops were successful and the harvest was safely in. Other peoples who relied on fishing for food developed rituals to try to make sure of a plentiful catch.

Food is a necessity of life, but it also forms a part of many celebrations. Feasts are held to

celebrate
the food itself, as in
harvest festivals the world over. But feasting
is also a way of celebrating special occasions
such as birthdays and weddings, religious
festivals like Christmas, and the existence of
family and friends.

From earliest times, people realized that
having a healthy body could not be taken
for granted. Any number of things could
go wrong, and very often did. Life was
hazardous for the early hunter-gatherers. If
they were not attacked by wild animals or
each other, they stood a fair chance of eating
something that would poison them or of
dying in childbirth. To find ways of curing
illness, people devised all sorts of weird and
wonderful cure-alls, often consisting of local
herbs and the magic spells and potions of
witch doctors and medicine men.

Once people had
begun to settle down and live together in
communities, getting along together became
another important part of life. Giving gifts is a
mark of respect and a sign of affection. All
levels of society exchange gifts, from the
lavish official gifts for visiting Heads of State
to simpler gifts such as cards and flowers.

However, people do not always live
together in harmony and mutual respect, and
then disputes arise. In order to survive, people
have had to find ways of sorting out
differences of opinion, from fights between
individuals to full-blown wars.

In this book, we look at rituals and
customs around the world and see that not
only are people's needs the same all over the
world, but their ways of dealing with needs
and celebrating successes are very similar too.

Hunting

In some parts of the world today, people live as they have for thousands of years. They rely on hunting and on gathering plants which grow wild for food. Imagine being trapped without food on a desert island or on a snowy mountain or in a tropical jungle. How would you cope?

People today at least have the benefit of knowledge. They know which animals are which and most have a reasonable idea what is edible and what is not. They know about the tools that people use and the materials needed to make them. But imagine if you appeared on Earth without any of this knowledge....

Where would you begin? Instinct would tell you that you had to search for food. But you would have to find ways of hunting successfully, which would involve stalking your prey and then somehow killing it.

People do not have sharp teeth and claws like meat-eating animals. They soon found that they needed help in the form of sharp tools for stabbing, cutting and skinning. They also had to kill the prey before it escaped or killed them. They learned to track their prey using footprints and tell-tale signs such as broken branches.

Animals use scent to warn them of danger, so the early hunters learned to keep down wind of their prey so that it could not smell them. They learned where animals went at different times of year by following them.

Plants may seem an easier and safer option, but only if you can look up the poisonous ones in a book! We cannot know how many people died or were taken ill while finding

HUNTER-GATHERERS, LIKE *the Pigmy peoples of Zaire and Cameroons, move from area to area as each location is exhausted of game and fruits. Usually women gather roots, leaves and fruits, while the men hunt.*

The Earliest Lifestyle

The ancestors of human beings began wrestling with these problems as early as four million years ago. There is evidence to show that early forms of people, known as 'hominids', had evolved in Africa by this time. They could stand upright and were feeding on small animals and plants from the forests where they lived.

By about tthree million years ago, these hominids had begun to fashion simple tools to help them catch and prepare their food . The earliest tools were simply sharp stones which they used to skin animals and cut up the meat. But as time went by, the hominids realized that they could make tools by shaving flakes off a stone to leave a sharp edge. This was the beginning of the period known as the 'Palaeolithic' or Old Stone Age and it lasted until about 12,000 BC.

out which plants were edible, but in the end they learned. Many of the plants which we grow today come from the ones identified by these early hunter-gatherers, and developed by the first farmers who planted seeds from the edible plants.

Depending on such a risky way of survival, it is no surprise that these early hunter-gatherers took comfort in rituals to help them out. Rituals involved with a successful hunt date back thousands of years, and some of these are still performed today.

People lived by hunting and gathering for nearly two million years before some of them began to settle into communities and farm the land. We know very little about the rituals they followed, if any, during this time.

Then, about 1,500,000 years ago, a new species of Stone Age people began to appear. Known as *Homo erectus*, these people were more intelligent than their predecessors and learned to hunt large animals such as elephants and bison by trapping them. It is thought that these hunters worked in groups, rounding animals up and driving them into bogs or over cliffs to trap or wound them. It would then be a simpler task to finish them off with stone tools.

The Neanderthal (or New Stone Age) people who lived in western Asia and Europe between 100,000 and 30,000 years ago, were probably the first to develop rituals concerned with hunting. Bears seem to have been particularly important to them. Bones and skulls have been found in caves where Neanderthal people sheltered. The way that these bones were arranged suggests that they were used in some sort of ritual.

Painting in the Caves

By about 30,000 years ago, people began to have enough time to spare from hunting and survival to begin to express themselves in artistic form. This was a great step forward which separated people from other animals.

The earliest forms of art were paintings on the walls of caves. These pictures, which mostly show animals like bison, mammoths and bears, give us some of our biggest clues about Stone Age hunters and their prey. But why did the hunters paint the animals they tracked and killed? Was it simply a need to record the world around them, or were the paintings part of some ritual?

The position of the paintings gives us some answers. A painting which was supposed to be decorative would normally be in a place where there was plenty of light, so that everyone could see it easily. Yet many of the cave paintings are tucked away in the darkest parts of the caves and are often difficult to get at. This suggests that they have some extra meaning beyond decoration.

SOME OF THE *earliest carvings, dating from more than 20,000 years ago, show game animals that the carvers would have hunted and the predators that they encountered during the hunt.*

Various theories have been put forward about how these pictures were used. One is that the hunters taught younger members of the tribe by showing them the animals and how to find and kill them. Some of the pictures show hunters as well as animals. The paintings in the Lascaux cave in France are about 15,000 years old. They are some of the most dramatic and vivid examples of cave art that have been found. One painting shows a bison which has been killed with a spear. A bison was a large and dangerous animal for a man armed only with spears and arrows. This painting may simply have been a record of a successful hunt, but in it, a dead man lies on the ground nearby, so perhaps it was intended to remind everyone that the hunter can be killed as easily as his prey.

The dark and secret positions of many cave paintings also suggest that they were part of some magic ritual concerned with the success of the hunt. The animals shown are often those that were hardest to find. The hunters may have thought that if they drew a particular animal before they went hunting, that animal would then surely appear. Many of the animals have spears or arrows in their bodies. Pictures also have marks and dents around them, as though stones and other missiles have been hurled at the walls. This suggests that the whole procedure of producing the paintings may have been a ritual 'hunt', carried out to ensure the success of the real hunt.

Desert Paintings

The Sahara Desert in Africa is the largest desert on Earth. In some parts of the Sahara, rain does not fall for years on end – nothing can grow on its sandy wastes. Yet there is evidence that this was not always the case. In the middle of the desert is a large range of rocky mountains called the Tassili. The rocks are completely bare of vegetation, yet valleys between them look like the paths of ancient rivers and streams. This suggests that the land was once well-watered so that plants grew and people could live there.

The most fascinating evidence for this theory is paintings on the rocks themselves. People sheltered in caves and under rocky overhangs in the mountains, and decorated these dwellings with paintings of animals such as rhinoceros, hippopotami, gazelles and giraffes. The people also kept domestic animals such as cattle, which are shown with collars around their necks and herdsmen standing with them. Other scenes show hunters with bows and arrows, and people dancing.

We do not know who these people were or exactly when they lived, but experts believe that the earliest of these pictures were painted about 5,000 years ago. By then, Egypt and Mesopotamia had already developed civilizations.

The Inuit

When the Spanish arrived in America in the late fifteenth and early sixteenth centuries, they found a land populated by millions of people who had no idea that the rest of the world existed. Evidence suggests that the ancestors of these people crossed overland from Siberia to the Americas between 30,000 and 15,000 years ago. They came across a land-bridge known as 'Beringia', which disappeared under the sea about 12,000 years ago, as the water level rose after the last Ice Age.

The people settled in different parts of America and formed their own separate lifestyles. The groups who settled in the northern areas of Alaska and the Canadian Arctic had to survive intense cold. The land

Tools for the Job

Some of the rituals concerned with the Inuit hunt were marks of respect for the victim. Hunters were always well aware of the difficulties in tracking down their prey and admired the skill of animals as they avoided the hunter. The Inuit believed that the soul of an animal respected a hunter more if it was hunted with a beautifully made weapon. They also thought that the soul of a dead animal was passed on to an unborn creature, and with it the knowledge of how it had been treated. So they took great care with their harpoons. The heads were superbly crafted from bone and were often decorated with carved designs. The small harpoon head (above) is for hunting seals. The large harpoon head is for whales.

was covered with snow and the seas were icy. Few mammals could live in these conditions, and the people learned to rely on seals, whales and other prey from the sea.

These people, now known as the Inuit, were better adapted than anyone in the world for living in icy conditions. Although the Inuit today have modern amenities to provide shelter and warmth, they survived by traditional methods for hundreds of years. Their traditional home was the 'igloo', a domed hut made from blocks of snow. They used skins to make warm clothes, and they hunted for food, travelling on sledges pulled by dogs, and killing their prey with harpoons.

The simplest harpoons had barbs on the shaft to hold the prey once speared. But in about 700 BC, a new weapon, known as the toggling harpoon, was introduced for hunting whales. It had a hinged head which lodged in the whale's blubber and stayed there. With this, the Inuit people became expert whalers. A group of scouts searched for whales among the ice floes in skin boats called 'kayaks'. Then, the harpooners moved in for the kill in large hide boats known as 'uniaks'.

American Hunters

In other parts of North America, the bison was the main prey for the hunters. Huge herds of bison roamed the great plains of central North America, which stretched from Alaska to the Gulf of Mexico.

The Native peoples of the Great Plains hunted in groups, and developed cunning methods of luring the animals into their traps. Some of these Native Americans dressed in animal skins and horns to fool the bison into thinking they were part of the herd. These imposters, bellowing like the animals themselves, slowly lured some of the bison into an enclosed area such as a gulch where the hunters could pounce.

The summer reunion was an important time for all of the tribes. This was when marriages were arranged, people exchanged tools and other goods, and rituals and dances were held to ensure that the hunting would be successful.

The 'shaman', or medicine man, played a central part in these rituals. Archaeologists have found evidence of ceremonial areas near the bison-trapping corrals. The shaman may have sat here, supervising the building of the structure and calling on the spirits to bring a successful hunt.

The shaman was highly respected and even feared among the people. He was their link with the spirit world of their ancestors. Before a hunt, the shaman carried out a ritual buffalo dance, acting out the creation legends, and celebrating the bison. The shaman recited magic spells in the form of songs, and the hunters had to go through various initiation rites to prepare them for the task ahead.

Sometimes the shaman acted out rituals to find the best place to hunt. The Mistassini Cree people had a special 'shaking tent' ritual to locate game. The shaman went into the specially constructed tent and sang about the hunt, making the tent poles shake as he did so. The way that the poles shook gave the shaman clues about the best direction for the hunters to go. Some tribes also had drumming ceremonies which helped the hunters decide where to go. The drums were said to have called up spirits who then guided the hunters to their destination.

•The Baka Pygmies of Central Africa•

In some parts of the world, people still live by hunting and gathering. Such peoples include tribes of Amazonian Indians from the rainforests of South America and the Pygmies of Central Africa who live in small groups in the forests of Cameroon, the Congo, the Central African Republic and Zaire.

The Pygmies were the original inhabitants of Central Africa until a taller farming people, the Bantu, arrived about 2,500 years ago. Gradually, the Bantu farmers took over from the Pygmy hunter-gatherers. Pygmy tribes learned to speak the Bantu language, and their own languages have disappeared.

The Baka Pygmies, who live in south-east Cameroon and the northern forests of the Congo basin, have remained more isolated than other tribes. They live in small groups of twenty-five to forty people, hunting animals such as antelope with spears and dogs. There is a Baka taboo (something forbidden by religious belief) that no man may eat meat that he has killed himself. Manhood comes by hunting and killing an animal. No member of a boy's family may eat any meat from his first kill. The next animal he kills can be shared between all his family except the boy and his father. Finally, only the boy cannot eat. He is now a man.

Before a young man can marry, he must prove his hunting skills by giving the bride's family meat from an animal he has killed. This proves that he can look after their daughter in the approved Baka style. He must hunt for his wife's family until his first child is born, after which he can take his family back to his own group.

Every night, the people sit round a fire in the dying light, and discuss the day's hunting and other events.

Older group members tell the younger ones age-old Baka legends. Advice is also given about settling disputes and living a good life. This is an important part of Baka tradition because there is no single leader of their tribe.

But things are changing. The Baka follow their hunter-gatherer lifestyle for about half the year, but for the other half, they live in semi-permanent camps near Bantu villages and work as labourers.

THE MEN HUNT *in groups, but only one makes the final kill, so that the others can eat. A boy proves that he is a man by hunting and killing an animal.*

·The Aboriginals·

Before the first ships of European settlers arrived in Australia in 1788, the country was populated by native people known as Aboriginals who had migrated there from south-east Asia about 20,000 years earlier. There were probably about 300,000 Aboriginals when the Europeans arrived. They were divided into about 500 semi-nomadic tribes who lived by hunting and gathering. Each group moved about within a set territory and operated in a highly organized way.

Religion was the most important way of maintaining aboriginal traditions and the rules by which they lived. They believed that certain mythical beings, some in human and some in animal form, had shaped the landscape and created the people who lived in it. The Aboriginals believed in an everlasting spiritual life, known as 'Eternal Dreaming'. Their religious beliefs inspired their music, poetry, sculpture and the rock paintings which can still be seen today. The land was so important to the Aboriginals that many of their religious rituals were bound up in it. Although they were not farmers, they relied on the plants and animals which they found for food.

Australia is the largest island in the world, and the climate is very varied. In the north, there are tropical forests, but much of the centre of the country is desert with scrubby vegetation. There is a dry and a wet season, but the rainfall is sporadic. In some desert areas, it does not rain for years and very little can grow. The weather was very important to the Aboriginals, and many of their most sacred rituals were concerned with the fertility of the land and the renewal of plants each year.

During the dry season from April to September, when the centre of the country is parched, the people had to rely on hunting for their food. They used spears, clubs and boomerangs. In the wet season, there were plants to gather, so they could stay in camps and pick berries and vegetables to add to their diet of meat and fish.

There are about 100,000 Aboriginals in Australia today, and some still live in the traditional way, though rifles have largely replaced the original weapons of the hunters.

Dividing the Spoils

When a hunt has been successful, there is the problem of dividing up the kill. Hunters usually work together in a group, and most have families to feed. So how should the meat be divided fairly?

Most hunter-gatherer groups have methods and rituals for deciding who has what from the kill. For example, if one hunter has been particularly brave or skilful, he may be due some special treatment. Or the meat may be divided according to who has the most mouths to feed.

The Guayaki people who live in the tropical forests of Paraguay have a similar custom to the Baka Pygmies. A hunter may not eat meat which he has caught himself. The Guayaki believe that a man who eats meat he has killed will become unlucky in hunting. However, this custom makes sense because it ensures that the hunter cannot claim all the meat for himself and his family. The kill is shared fairly between all the people in the group, but the hunter himself must depend on someone else to kill meat for him.

The !Kung people are hunter-gatherers who live in the Kalahari Desert in southern Africa. They are part of a group known as the San, or 'Bushmen' of the Kalahari. The desert is not as arid as the Sahara, and a surprising amount of plant life manages to survive.

The women use their digging sticks to collect juicy tubers which provide moisture as well as food. Meanwhile, the men go out to hunt antelope and other animals which will then be shared out among the group.

In the evening, the hunters return to their temporary camp to talk and boast of their feats of tracking and marksmanship. They will also sing and tell stories around the fire.

HERE, !KUNG HUNTERS *are carving up an antelope. The meat will be divided among the group by a complex ritual of gift-giving. Hunter-gatherers' strong beliefs about sharing meat are designed to prevent anyone from getting greedy when meat is in short supply.*

The Masai People

The Masai people who live in Kenya and Tanzania are cattle-herders who lead a semi-nomadic life, finding grass for their animals. Cattle are a sign of status and wealth among the Masai, who also keep smaller animals for meat. The men herd and look after the cattle. The women milk the cows and prepare the dish of curdled milk and blood which is the men's staple diet.

Young Masai boys go through an initiation ceremony, after which they become members of the 'moran' or warrior class. The moran were once the Masai's army, and they are still regarded as defenders of the tribe. After initiation, a boy first becomes a junior warrior. As more boys become junior warriors, the older ones are promoted to senior warriors. The warriors live outside the village and are not allowed to marry. Senior warriors finally become elders who may marry and raise a family. The best of these become leaders of the various groups.

Masai warriors are expected to be brave and fearless hunters, although they do not rely on hunting for food. One test of courage is the traditional lion hunt, though lions are now becoming so scarce, and are often only to be found in reserves, that the hunt is not practised as frequently as it once was.

MASAI LION HUNT

There are traditional rituals governing the decoration of shields, the use of head-dresses, and the trophies that are handed out at the end of the hunt.

SYMBOLS OF BRAVERY
Each warrior carries a shield made of buffalo hide. The shield is decorated with symbols showing which section of the tribe the warrior belongs to. Warriors who have carried out acts of particular bravery are allowed to include special circular patterns.

LION DANCE
Before the hunt begins, the warriors perform ritual dances, including the 'Namba', in which the dancers jump up in the air and land stiff-legged. As they come down, they make sounds that are supposed to sound like a lion coughing.

GETTING READY
The hunters gather. Most wear head-dresses made from ostrich feathers, but hunters who have held the tail of a lion in an earlier hunt may wear a lion's-mane head-dress. The hunters move off together to look for lions in the scrub.

THE SUCCESSFUL HUNTERS
After a kill, the warriors gather round the lion and decide who deserves a trophy. The bravest hunters are given the lion's mane, tail and paws.

Ancient Greece

Ancient religions show the importance of hunting and the relationship between people and animals. The ancient Greeks worshipped many gods, including Artemis, goddess of hunting.

In Greek mythology, Artemis was the daughter of Zeus and Leto, and the twin sister of Apollo. Apollo is usually shown as a beautiful young man who was the god of hunting, but also of healing, music and poetry. Artemis is portrayed as a huntress with a bow and arrow. She is sometimes dressed in hunting clothes, with young animals, and sometimes with horns in the shape of crescent moons as she was also in charge of the moon.

By the time of Homer's *Odyssey*, Artemis was known as the virgin goddess running through the woods and fields in pursuit of wild boar and stags. But Artemis was not a kindly goddess who helped the hunters. On the contrary, she had a fearsome temper and several myths show the ways in which she took revenge on those who crossed her. She could not bear to be seen by mortals, so hunters were afraid to go into the forests in case they stumbled upon her by accident.

One myth tells what might happen to them if they did. A hunter called Actaeon lost his way in the forest and came across Artemis bathing in a pool. She was so furious that he had seen her naked that she turned him into a stag. Actaeon's own hounds then chased the stag and tore it to pieces. Such dire misfortune must have given hunters a healthy respect for the forests and the dangers of getting lost when Artemis was about.

The Story of Niobe

Another myth which shows that Artemis was not be taken lightly is the story of Niobe, wife of Amphion, king of Thebes, who had seven sons and seven daughters. Niobe was unwise enough to crow over Leto, boasting that she had fourteen wonderful children when Leto had only two.

Leto was so furious that she summoned Artemis and Apollo to get rid of all Niobe's children. Armed with bow and arrows and his deadly aim, Apollo first shot the boys one by one.

Niobe, arriving on the scene with her daughters around her, was enraged and shouted that her children still surpassed those of Leto. For an answer, Artemis drew her bow and shot the daughters. As she shot the youngest daughter, Niobe sank down, turned to stone by her sorrow. Only her tears still flowed.

Hunting for Sport

Even when people had settled in one place and begun to farm, the tradition of hunting still continued, and eventually it became a sport. In the Middle Ages, Europe was largely covered with forests where deer and wild pigs lived. European kings enjoyed hunting – they would set off on horseback with their court to kill a stag or wild boar which could then be eaten. But the fun was in the chase and boasting about the kill.

Hunting for sport is still popular today. Hunters track deer or shoot birds, following the methods used by their hunter-gatherer ancestors. They follow tracks and use dogs to pick up scents. People known as beaters are sometimes employed to surround the quarry and force it out into the open.

Fox-hunting is supposedly carried out to keep down the numbers of foxes, which are pests to farmers. But it is enjoyed as a sport in which the fox is chased by hunters on horseback and a pack of hounds. The huntsmen and women ride across country, following the hounds. If the hounds catch the fox, they will kill it, often by tearing it apart.

Fox-hunting is dangerous. The horses gallop flat out across fields, jumping over any obstacles in their way, and riders can be thrown off and killed. Many people nowadays think that fox-hunting is cruel and that there must be more humane ways of culling foxes.

Fishing is a very popular sport in Europe and North America – both with bait and using a 'fly'. There are also people who hunt using birds of prey. This was popular in the Middle Ages in Europe, but nowadays the most skilled hunters come from Arabia.

THESE DEER HUNTERS *in Scotland have followed age-old methods to track down their quarry. They know all about the deer, where they are likely to be and what they are likely to do, and they can follow tell-tale signs such as tracks and scents.*

Planting

When people began to settle down and farm the land about 12,000 years ago, their priorities changed. Growing crops was a year-long cycle which required the right conditions – fertile soil and good weather.

The ancient civilizations who began to farm the land soon realized that this was not an easy option. The earliest of them, the Mesopotamians and the Egyptians, lived near rivers where the climate was hot. Sunshine was not a problem but water was. They relied on the rains which only came at certain times of the year. If the rains did not come, the water level in the rivers sank, and the ground became as hard as rock. So each year was filled with worries. Would the rains come? Would the sun shine? Would the river flood and make the land on its banks more fertile?

Their fears that things would not go according to plan led to the establishment of new religions with gods who they could turn to to sort everything out. Most ancient religions had a sun god and a rain god, sometimes also a god or goddess of fertility and a god for the staple crop.

The Aztecs settled in what is now Mexico. They called on a whole range of gods to help them survive. Two of the most important were Huitzilpochtli, the sun god, and Tlaloc, the god of rain. Chalchihuitlicue was the water goddess, while Chicomecoatl was responsible for the maize plant, and Ometochtli watched over the maguey cactus. Xipe Totec was the god of planting and spring. Much of the Aztecs' life was spent making sacrifices and carrying out rituals to please all these gods and ensure good crops.

A Lifeline for Egypt

The ancient Egyptians lived by the River Nile. To either side of the river lay endless stretches of desert. Nothing would grow there if it were not for the life-giving waters of the Nile.

In summer the Nile flooded, depositing rich, fertile mud all over the surrounding land. Over the years, mounds of mud built up along the banks of the river. Early settlers in Egypt built huts on the top of these mounds. When the river flooded, the villagers stayed safe in their huts above the water level. When the Nile receded, the people came out of their houses and planted their crops in the fertile mud, watering them with water hauled up from the basin reservoirs.

However in some years the rains did not come in Africa, and so the Nile did not flood. In other years, the river flooded so much that the villages were swept away. So the flooding of the Nile became an important part of Egyptian worship and ritual.

By about 3000 BC, the villages had become towns and cities, and Egypt was ruled by a pharaoh. The pharaoh was believed to be a god as well as a king, an earthly version of the sky god, Horus, and the son of the sun god, Ra. One legend explaining this belief was that Horus was the son of Osiris, a god of

IN ANCIENT EGYPT, *the pharaoh was seen as a god-king who controlled the whole universe.*

nature who controlled the ebb and flow of the Nile. Osiris had ruled Egypt, but he was murdered by his jealous brother Seth, who hacked his body apart and spread the pieces across the land. Osiris was resurrected by his sister-wife, Isis, who collected the parts and put them back together. He did not return to Earth, but became the god of the afterlife. After many bitter fights with Seth, Horus was finally proclaimed god-king of all Egypt.

When the pharaohs began to establish themselves as the new line of kings, people remembered the legend about Egypt being ruled by one god-king and concluded that each pharaoh was the human form of Horus come back to rule over them.

The pharaohs conducted elaborate rituals to ensure that the flood waters came to just the right level. People's working lives were also governed by the level of the river. While the flood waters were pouring over the land in the summer, and people could not work on the land, they worked for the pharaoh on building projects like the pyramids. When the waters receded, they went back to working in the fields.

The flooding of the Nile continued to govern the lives of people in Egypt until the 1960s, when the High Dam was built at Aswan to control the floods and store water for irrigation schemes.

Bringing the Rains

Many of the peoples who live in dry climates have developed rituals for bringing rains. The people who lived in the dry regions of North America such as New Mexico and Arizona used ceremonial dances, often based on ancient folk legends.

Many of the North American tribes performed some form of snake dance. Snakes were very important to the Hopi of Arizona because they were thought to bring the rain.

The Hopi had underground chambers with altars where they worshipped their rain god. On the altar was an image of the god with his snake and emblems to show wind, rain and storm. Live snakes for the ceremonies were kept in a separate chamber, known as the 'kisi'. The snake dance ceremony lasted for sixteen days, and the dancers carried the snakes about with them during this time.

Among traditional societies in Africa, people believed that 'medicine men' or 'witch doctors' had the power to bring the rain. So powerful were the medicine men that they were usually also chiefs of their tribes. However, many of these chiefs took the precaution of building their villages on the slopes of high hills, no doubt because they had noticed that clouds form above hills, so there was a fair chance that their predictions of rain would be right.

In good years, when plenty of rain fell, people revered the chief because of his magical abilities, and he became rich and

powerful. But things did not always go so well. If there was a drought, the people could turn on the chief and kill him, thinking that the lack of rain was his fault.

This custom of killing or injuring a chief who failed to produce rain seems to have been fairly widespread among African societies. In some parts of West Africa, tribes made prayers and offerings to their chief to help him bring rain. If he failed, they tied him up with ropes and took him to the grave of his ancestors so that he could ask them to help him.

WHEN THE RAIN-MAKER wanted rain to fall, he plunged his rain-stones (crystals or amethysts) into water and then beckoned to the clouds with a piece of split cane, muttering spells. His gestures with the cane indicated whether the clouds should come nearer or go in another direction.

The Navaho Rain-making Chant

The Navaho people believe that drought can happen because people have had evil thoughts. Rain-making ceremonies can bring the drought to an end, but only if the rituals are performed correctly and the bad thoughts which caused the problem have been banished.

Part of the Navaho ceremony is a chant for rain which runs like this:

'The Rain Boy with the dark cloud feet,
He arises facing me....
The Rain Girl with the dark fog feet,
She arises facing me.'

•Sacrifices for the Crops•

Most rituals concerned with crop fertility were fairly harmless, but some peoples went to enormous lengths to make sure of a good harvest, even sacrificing humans so that their blood would enrich the fields.

One of the best known human sacrifice rituals was reported by British officers in India in the nineteenth century. The Khond tribe of Bengal offered sacrifices to the earth goddess in the hope that human blood would make the soil fertile and keep the crops free from disease. An important crop to the Khonds was the spice turmeric, and they thought that it would not get its deep red colour without the addition of blood.

The victim to be sacrificed was known as the 'Meriah'. Not everyone could have the dubious privilege of becoming a Meriah. The ritual would not work unless the Meriah had been bought for the purpose or was the descendant of another victim. Parents sometimes sold their children as potential Meriahs because it was regarded as an honourable way to die and one which would help the community as a whole.

The victims were not usually sacrificed at once. Some were kept for years before they met their fate. Children were not sacrificed until they were grown up, so they had plenty of time to look forward to their untimely end. When a Meriah boy reached adulthood, he was usually given a wife, another Meriah. They were given some land to farm and were encouraged to have children so as to increase the stock of future victims.

About two weeks before a victim was due to be sacrificed, his hair was cut off. On the day before the sacrifice, the Meriah was dressed in new clothes and led in a procession to a forest. He was tied to a tree and his body was anointed with melted butter and turmeric. All through the day, people came to pay their respects and to ensure their own good luck by taking something such as a hair

or a small smear of turmeric from the Meriah's body. The crowds danced and sang all through the night. The next day, the victim was anointed with oil, drugged and killed by strangling, crushing or slow roasting over a fire. The idea was to make him cry for as long as possible, for the more tears shed, the more rain would fall on the crops.

The body was then cut up, and representatives from each village took a piece home. In the village, the priest was waiting for the flesh, which he buried in a hole in the ground as an offering to the earth goddess. Each man in the village put some earth in the hole and poured in water from a gourd. The bones and other remains of the victim were burned and the ashes were scattered on the fields.

The British were horrified by this practice when they discovered what was going on, and put a stop to it in the nineteenth century. Yet to the Khonds, the unfortunate Meriah had magical powers which could influence the earth goddess and bring a successful harvest.

•From Winter to Summer•

In temperate areas such as Europe and North America, the changing seasons were all-important. The change from winter to spring meant that the plants could begin to grow again. Some rituals carried out at this time of year involved mock battles between winter and summer.

In Sweden, for example, May Day celebrations used to include a battle between two troops of men on horseback. One side was led by 'Winter', who was dressed in furs and threw snowballs and ice to make the cold weather last longer. The other side was led by 'Summer', dressed in leaves and flowers – they threw petals and leaves. The ritual battle always ended with the victory of Summer over Winter, and everyone celebrated with a feast afterwards.

A similar battle was acted out in parts of Germany. After a tough fight, 'Summer', dressed in ivy, finally managed to defeat 'Winter', who wore a casing of straw. The defeated 'Winter' was thrown on the ground and his straw casing was torn off him and scattered around. Meanwhile, supporters from both sides sang songs celebrating Summer's victory over Winter. Then everyone went from house to house collecting gifts of produce such as eggs.

It used to be the custom in many parts of Europe to call up the tree spirits in spring or early summer. Villagers would go to the woods and cut down a tree which was brought back and set up on the village green or some other space. It was believed that the tree brought the blessings of the tree spirits to the village, and this would help new plants to grow well. The branches were cut from the tree, and it was decked with flowers and ribbons. Then, the people danced around it as part of the May Day celebrations.

In many places, the tree was not removed after May Day. Instead, it was left on the village green until a new tree was brought the following May. In England, the tradition of dancing around the maypole continued long after the custom of bringing in the tree spirits

'GREEN GEORGE' REPRESENTED *a tree spirit in May Day celebrations.*

had been forgotten, and the maypole became a permanent fixture on village greens. It is still carried out as part of folk dancing demonstrations.

Sometimes the tree spirit was represented by a person. In parts of eastern Europe, young people would deck a tree with garlands of flowers and carry it in a procession led by the 'Green George'. This character was dressed from head to foot in green birch branches. At the end of the ceremony, the

IN GERMANY, THE *flower-crowned May Queen would lead a troop of young women and children through the streets to welcome the spring.*

man playing the Green George stepped quickly out of his greenery so that no one spotted him, and an effigy was put in his place. This effigy was thrown into a pond or river to ensure that rain would fall to water the crops. Sometimes 'Green George' was thrown in himself.

The spirit of spring was often known as the 'May King' or 'May Queen'. In parts of Germany, the boys of the village raced to the maypole and the one who got there first became the May King. A garland of flowers was put around his neck, and he led a procession around the houses, singing songs to wish everyone good luck and asking for gifts of fresh produce. Germany also had a tradition of appointing a May Queen in some places. This was a young girl who wore a white dress and a crown of spring flowers. She led a wild procession of young women around the town or village. They danced and swirled round her continuously, singing all the time. The May festivities were carried out in many parts of Europe.

Planting Ceremonies

The planting of certain crops may be accompanied by ritual, particularly if the crop is a staple food. Rice is such an important crop in the Far East that there are rituals for planting and for harvesting it.

In southern India, for example, there was a tradition among the Burgher tribe that the first handful of seed must be sown by a man from the Curumbar tribe. The Burghers regarded these people as sorcerers so it was thought to be good luck for one of them to plant the new crop.

In Sumatra and Java, people believe that the rice is guarded by a female spirit called 'Saning Sari', or 'Rice-mother'. Before the rice is sown, the best grains are chosen to represent the Rice-mother. The woman who sows these grains in the nursery bed lets her hair hang loose and takes a ritual bath afterwards so that there will be a good harvest. The Rice-mother plant has to be nurtured as it grows, because if it dies, the harvest will fail. When it is time to transplant the rice, the Rice-mother is put in a special part of the field and prayers are said to it, such as:

'Saning Sari, may you be frightened neither by lightning nor by passers-by...'

THE RICE-TRANSPLANTING CEREMONY
A traditional ceremony for the transplanting of rice is held every year in some rural parts of Japan. The ceremony takes place on the first Sunday in June in honour of the crop which has been the staple food in Japan for more than two thousand years.

The ceremony more or less died out when the feudal system of imperial Japan was abolished in 1900. It was revived in some places in 1930, and the Japanese government now encourages people to hold the ceremony.

FLOWER COSTUMES
Dancers wearing enormous hats decorated with arches of flowers process through the streets.

DANCES FOR THE SPIRITS
Children act out dances that tell of legendary events. These were originally intended to amuse and entertain the spirits of the Shinto religion.

A GREAT PROCESSION
In the middle of the day, there is a procession that includes oxen carrying silver and gold-coloured saddles and banners showing their owners' family emblems.

PRAYERS BY SMOKE
Women pray before a fire of rice straw to summon the rice god Sanbai-sama. The smoke is supposed to carry their prayers towards heaven.

PLANTING
The women bend down to plant the rice seedlings. Guided by a length of cord stretched across the field, they work in a perfectly straight line, and do everything at exactly the same time. In the background, musicians play on pipes and drums as the women work.

Harvest

The harvest has always been a crucial time for people who farm. Even in modern industrialized societies, where food can be preserved, stored and transported far more easily than before, a poor harvest may lead to shortages and make everyday items more expensive. But in many parts of the world, a bad harvest leads to famine. This has always been the case throughout history. If there was not enough food to go around, people would starve.

R ituals were developed to please the gods, because it was thought that if the gods were happy, they would be more likely to make the crops grow well. There were also rituals to give thanks after a good harvest. Some of these are still carried out today.

Europe

Harvest rituals often took place in the fields as the crops were being cut. In Europe, the cutting of the last sheaf was particularly symbolic. The last sheaf was thought to contain the power of the harvest, and it was regarded as a great honour to cut it. The task was often performed by a young woman who became the 'Harvest Queen'. She was decked in garlands of flowers and helped up on the wagon to ride home with the last load. The people followed the load home in a procession, ringing handbells and cheering and shouting in triumph.

At harvest time, farmers had to take on extra helpers to cut the crops as quickly as possible, because a downpour of rain could ruin them. The farm hands appointed one of their number to be the chief reaper and negotiate with the farmer for good conditions and rates of pay. This leader became the Lord of the Harvest. The Lady of the Harvest was in fact a man dressed up as a woman, a role taken by the second most important reaper.

The Lord and Lady of the Harvest rode home seated on top of the last load. This was a very dubious privilege, because it was customary to throw buckets of water over the load to ensure rain for the next season's crops! Customs like this were a way of letting off steam at the end of a year of hard farmwork.

THE OLD ENGLISH *custom of twisting the last sheaf of corn into a corn dolly was said to keep the spirit of the corn alive throughout the winter. People believed that if the spirit was not kept alive until the next crop was sown, the corn would die, and there would not be a good harvest. The corn dolly, which was sometimes given a name such as 'The Old Wife' or 'Granny', was made in the field as soon as the last corn had been cut.*

Although the tradition dates back to pre-Christian times, the corn dolly was often taken into church for the harvest festival. Corn dollies are still made, but this is to keep a rural craft alive rather than to preserve the corn spirit.

The Corn Spirit

Many communities made the spirit of the corn more permanent by twisting the last sheaf into a figure of some kind. In England, the last sheaf was used to make the figure of a woman which was known as a 'corn dolly'. The doll was dressed in women's clothes and taken to the harvest supper, where it sat in a place of honour at the table. After the supper, the corn doll was hung up in the barn or the farmhouse as a good luck symbol for the next year's harvest.

This tradition probably dates back to the Greek goddess, Demeter who was thought to restore life to the Earth every spring. The Romans called her Ceres. Other corn models, such as horns of plenty, were made at harvest time and called corn dollies.

In Ireland, people still make harvest knots from lengths of straw twisted into various shapes. In the past, lovers exchanged the knots as a sign of their commitment to one another. The girl wore the knot in her hair, and the man pinned his to his coat.

The spirit of the corn was represented in different ways in other parts of Europe. In France and Germany, for example, it was seen as a wolf or a dog which lurked in the last sheaf. The reapers cutting the last sheaf were said to be 'catching the wolf'. The wolf was not a benevolent spirit. Children were afraid to go into the cornfields in case the wolf got them, a fear no doubt encouraged by farmers who did not want their crop trampled on. The corn spirit was also represented by a cat, a goat, a pig or a hare in different regions.

Jewish First Fruits

Several Jewish festivals were originally harvest celebrations, although they have now taken on additional significance.

'Shavuot', or the Festival of Weeks, takes place at the end of the barley harvest and the beginning of the wheat harvest in May or June. It was once held to give thanks for the crops, but it also marks the time when God gave Moses the 'Torah', or books of law, on Mount Sinai, and the festival commemorates that event, too. The Torah consists of the first books of the Jewish Bible, or Old Testament of the Christian Bible. During Shavuot, homes and synagogues are decorated with fresh fruit and flowers, and there are readings from the Torah.

'Succoth', the Festival of Tabernacles or Booths, takes place at the time of the grape

SUCCOTH

During Succoth, many families build a booth or shelter in the garden of their home. The booth is made from branches, twigs and leaves, and is big enough to hold a table. The inside is decorated with fruit and flowers, and families eat their meals there during the seven days of the festival.

In the past, families lived in the booths for the festival, sleeping, worshipping and celebrating there. The booths are traditionally built so that the night sky can be seen through the roof, to remind people how frail they are compared with the vast universe.

harvest. People give thanks to God for the fruits of garden and field, but they also remember the long and dramatic history of the people of Israel. Families build a simple booth in the garden in memory of how their ancestors wandered in the desert.

Four plants – palm, citron, myrtle and willow – are especially significant at this time, because they have characteristics which demonstrate the difference between people in the world. For example, the sharp taste and fragrant scent of citron symbolizes people who are learned and carry out good deeds. Myrtle, on the other hand, is fragrant but has no taste, so it symbolizes people who have little learning but are good to others.

These festivals are celebrated on the same days in Jewish communities all over the world, although they are only actually harvest times in Israel.

Rice Harvests

In the Far East, there are many rituals for protecting the soul of the rice. In Malaysia, elaborate rituals surround the birth of the 'Baby Rice Soul' at harvest time. The first step is to banish evil spirits by burning rubbish and foul-smelling herbs to drive them away. A magician then chooses seven stalks of rice which are cut and wrapped in a shawl like a baby. The Baby Rice Soul is taken to the farmer's house, where it is treated like a real baby.

For three days after the birth of the Baby Rice Soul, only one small basket of rice can be harvested on each day. The rice is cut by one reaper who works in silence and must make sure that his shadow does not fall across the plants. On the seventh day after the birth

Indonesia

In Indonesia, the rice growing in the field is treated like a pregnant woman. People believe that any sudden shock will prevent the rice from producing grain, so no guns can be fired in the field, and there must be no talk of death or demons.

of the Baby Rice Soul, the real harvest can begin because the rice soul is now protected.

In Sumatra and Java, the Rice-mother, which was chosen when the crop was sown, has disappeared from view by harvest time, and a new one has to be chosen. When the rice is ready to be cut, the oldest woman in the family goes to choose the Rice-mother which must be the first stalks that bend in the breeze. The chosen stalks are tied together but left standing until the first of the rice has been cut and served in a festive meal. Then, the Rice-mother is brought home under an umbrella, and put into the barn where she looks after the rice as it is harvested.

On the island of Buru, in the East Indies, there was a tradition known as 'eating the soul of the rice' at harvest time. Every

ON SUMATRA, THE *oldest woman of the family ties the rice stalks together to make the Rice-mother.*

member of the group had to contribute some of their newly harvested rice. Some of the rice was set aside as an offering to the spirits, and the rest was eaten at a special meal.

On Sulawesi in Indonesia, the first rice was traditionally picked by the priest. He roasted the grains and ground them into meal which was shared out among all the households. Sometimes the women did the grinding. The women cooked the rice and took it back to the priest with an egg which was offered to the spirits. After the priest had made the offering, he gave the rice back to the women so that all the family could eat some of it.

•Fishing Rituals•

People who rely on fishing for their survival have also developed traditional rituals to make sure of a good catch. Fishing can be a very unpredictable way of getting food. Floods or droughts can affect the number of fish found in a river, and people who fish in the world's seas can easily fall victim to storms.

Some Native American fishing customs are interesting. The people who live in British Columbia in Canada hunted there because the seas and rivers were alive with fish. But in some years, the fish did not arrive on time, so a wizard was employed to make an image of a swimming fish and put it in the water, facing in the direction the fish usually came from. The people believed that this would make the fish arrive quickly.

Other rituals were concerned with respecting the wishes of the fish and not upsetting them, even though they were due to be caught and eaten. The Kwakiuti people live in the coastal regions of British Columbia where salmon is the main catch. They believe that when a salmon dies, its soul goes to a salmon country where it is born again to return the next year. But the salmon can only be reborn if the bones and offal from its body are thrown into the sea. If the bones are burned, the soul is killed.

The Huron people who lived near the St Lawrence River also believed that burning fish bones would destroy future supplies. They thought that the soul of the fish would warn other fish not to go anywhere near the Hurons because they would burn their bones. The Hurons also had a special preacher who entreated the fish to come into the fishermen's nets. After supper each day, the people would stand around in silence as the preacher came up with every argument he could think of to persuade the fish to come into the traps. Most important was his assurance that the Huron were good people who did not burn fish bones, so the fish should not be afraid of their fate, but should swim courageously into the fishermen's nets.

The people of Peru in South America worshipped the most plentiful fish as gods, because they believed that the first fish of each species was created in heaven and gave birth to all the other fish of that type. Each group of people worshipped the type of fish that was most plentiful in their area. Some

PEOPLE WHO RELY *on fish for their food know that the fish will not always do their bidding, so they have devised rituals to try and make sure of a good catch.*

worshipped sardines, while others prayed to skate, dogfish, crayfish, or even crabs if there was nothing better around to catch.

In some communities, fishermen must observe strict taboos during the fishing season. On the Caroline Islands in the South Pacific, fishermen are not allowed to go home during the fishing season which lasts for about eight weeks. When they are on shore, they must spend their time in the men's

clubhouse, and must not look at their wives or any other women during this time. If a fisherman does look a woman in the face, it is believed that the flying fish will gouge his eyes out at night. If his wife, or any female relation wants to bring him something, she must stand near the shore, with her back to the clubhouse. The fisherman can talk to her and take the gift she has brought him, provided he keeps his back to her all the time.

·Fishing Superstitions·

As well as rituals for catching fish, fishermen have many superstitions which they believe will help or hinder the catch. The river fisherman, for example, knows that he must not stop to count how many fish he has caught, or he will catch nothing more that day.

If a right-handed fisherman casts his line with his left hand, he might as well give up and go home, because the fish will not come near him. A similar fate awaits the left-handed fisherman who casts with his right hand. But good luck will befall the fisherman who spots an earwig on his way to fish, provided he remembers to cast his line properly, of course!

The Scottish solution on a day when the fish will not bite is to throw a fisherman into the water and then pull him out as though he is a catch. Perhaps this is designed to show the fish what is expected of them. Another old Scottish superstition among sea fishing communities is that it is very unlucky for a fisherman to say God's name. If anyone does this, the whole crew must touch a piece of

iron to avert the bad luck. Also the words 'pig', 'sow' or 'swine' must not be used when the nets are being lowered into the sea. If anyone utters these forbidden words, the whole catch will be lost unless the fishermen quickly touch the iron studs on their boots.

One of the best ways to make sure of a good catch is said to be for a fisherman and his wife to have a blazing row before he goes to sea. The row must start naturally, however, as it will not work if one partner goads the other into an argument deliberately. Any fisherman who meets a woman in a white apron on his way to his boat is doomed to failure. He can only cancel the bad luck by going home and waiting for the next tide.

Anglers, who are fishing for sport rather than for a living, have some superstitions of their own. It is very bad luck to change fishing rods in the middle of a fishing session. Bait should be spat on before being cast. And only a foolhardy angler sits on an upturned bucket as that is the best way of making sure that he will not catch anything.

There are also superstitions about the fish themselves. Fish in general are supposed to bring wisdom and knowledge to those who eat them. Sharks following a ship are seen as an omen that there will be a death on board during the voyage. Whales are not fish, but similar superstitions surround them. They are said to be lucky, and it is very bad luck to kill one. But if a whale is seen in a place where it does not usually go, that is an ill omen.

FROM THROWING THE *fisherman into the water to not sitting on an upturned bucket, fishermen the world over have superstitions about what will bring good and bad luck.*

Eating & Drinking

Food is such an essential aspect of life that eating has long been a major part of most celebrations. Perhaps early hunting communities celebrated when they had had a particularly good kill and there was more food than usual to go round. Certainly ancient civilizations regarded a 'groaning board' as a sign of wealth.

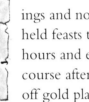 **K**ings and nobles sometimes held feasts that went on for hours and even days, with course after course served off gold plates, and music, dancing and singing to help the food and wine go down. But lowlier people also had celebrations, and food formed a part of these. Rites of passage such as births and weddings, and religious festivals in honour of the gods were all occasions – and excuses – for feasting.

Many food customs still survive today. When you sit down to a family meal, the way that the table is set and the order of the courses will probably be much the same as in other households. The utensils we use for cooking and eating vary from country to country, but each country has its standard way of doing things.

Good manners vary too. In Japan, Arabia and elsewhere, chewing noisily and burping are signs of appreciation for a good meal. There are also religious rituals concerning food. People of some religions may not eat certain foods. Other foods are served as part of religious festivals or services. In many cultures, it is traditional to give thanks for food, either by thanking the host or the cook, or by saying a prayer of thanks to God.

ALL OVER THE *world, food and drink have played a major part at festivals and celebrations since the time of the very first humans.*

Harvest Suppers

Once the harvest was safely in, the farmer and his wife laid on a feast for the reapers. Known as a 'Harvest Supper' or 'Harvest Home', this meal was traditionally served in a barn, which was decorated with garlands of flowers. The Harvest Home gave everyone a chance to make merry and enjoy themselves after the hard work of the harvest. The food at an English harvest home would probably include beef, plum pudding and plenty of beer. A traditional dish known as 'frumenty' might also be served. This was a milk pudding made with wheat, milk, raisins and currants, flavoured with sugar and spices.

The Pilgrim Fathers took some of these customs to America in the seventeenth century. In 1621, a group of settlers gathered to give thanks for the harvest. From then on, a celebration known as 'Thanksgiving' was held every year. President Lincoln set aside the last Thursday in November as Thanksgiving Day in the United States. This is an important day for American families, when everyone gets together for a traditional meal of roast turkey and pumpkin pie.

THE COW IS *sacred to Hindus, who do not eat its flesh. Cows are allowed to roam freely even in the major cities of India.*

Religious Rules

Some of the most well-known food customs come from the world's religions. Many are rules about what can and cannot be eaten. Jewish people have some of the strictest rules about food. They are only allowed to eat the meat of animals which have cloven hooves and chew the cud. This means they can eat the meat of cattle, sheep, goats and deer, but not pigs. Only the forequarters of the animal may be eaten.

Jews cannot eat shellfish, because only sea creatures with scales and fins are allowed. There are other rules about the preparation of the food. Meat and dairy foods must not be eaten at the same meal and must be prepared separately. Animals must be slaughtered in a certain way. All food is divided into 'kosher', or 'fit to eat', and 'trayf', or 'unclean'.

Hindus do not forbid the eating of meat, but they believe it is better not to kill and eat animals. Devout Hindus and 'Brahmans', who come from the priestly (highest) caste or class, are expected to be vegetarians, but some Hindus do eat meat. Beef, however, is strictly forbidden, because the cow is considered a sacred animal. This is possibly because, in India, the home of the Hindu religion, cows are worth more alive than dead. They provide milk to drink and oxen to pull ploughs.

Hindus also have strict rules about who may eat with whom. For example, a Brahman may not eat with or take food from an 'untouchable' who is from the lowest caste.

Muslim rules about food are laid down in their holy book, the 'Qur'an', in a section known as 'The Cow'. Muslims must not eat pork or blood, and they are not allowed to drink alcohol. Buddhists are strictly vegetarian as meat is forbidden in their religion. In the past, Roman Catholic Christians were not allowed to eat meat on Friday. This rule has been relaxed nowadays.

Some foods have a particular significance at religious feasts. The Jewish New Year is celebrated with bread and slices of apple dipped in honey as a symbol of sweetness. 'Yom Kippur', the Day of Atonement, is a day of fasting, but on the previous day people eat special pancakes filled with meat. Called 'kreplach', these are a symbol of stern judgements wrapped in mercy. The most important Jewish festival is 'Pesach' or Passover, which commemorates the escape from Egypt. No leavened, or raised, bread must be eaten during the eight days, so the staple food is flat wafers of unleavened bread called 'matzah'. On the first evening of Passover, there is a ritual family meal where everyone eats bitter herbs as a symbol of the suffering of Israelite slaves in Egypt.

Eggs, which symbolize spring and fertility, are given at Easter in Christian countries, although this custom probably dates back to pre-Christian times. In countries where Orthodox Christianity is followed, such as Russia and Greece, hard-boiled eggs are dyed red to represent Christ's blood. The eggs are broken open on Easter Sunday, symbolizing the opening of Christ's tomb.

Fasting

Fasting, or going without food, is another important religious ritual. The Muslim festival of Ramadan is a thirty-day fast commemorating the time when the prophet Mohammed was visited by the Angel Gabriel. All Muslims over the age of twelve must go without food or drink from dawn to sunset. They are allowed a light meal before dawn. At sunset, the day's fast ends with a call from the minaret of the mosque, and everyone has a special evening meal called 'iftar'.

The end of Ramadan is celebrated by eating sweets such as sugared almonds during a feast called 'Id-al-Fitir' or the Feast of Fast-breaking.

•The Significance of Salt•

No matter what their national diet is, people all over the world enjoy seasoning on their food, and one of the most widely used seasonings is salt. Salt, a mineral found in some rocks and in seawater, has been used for thousands of years as a means of adding extra flavour to bland food and also of preserving food.

IN THE SALT MINES

Salt miners working deep under the earth often carved sculptures in the salt as a sign of religious devotion. The most famous example is the Wieliczka mine near Krakow in Poland. More than 100 metres below ground is a maze of tunnels which have been cut by miners since the eleventh century.

In the tunnels, there are underground shrines, statues of saints and complete religious scenes all cut from the salt. Today, this extraordinary mine is a tourist attraction and underground leisure centre, with its own ballroom and tennis court.

Salt can be extracted from rock by mining, or obtained by evaporating seawater. Some of the oldest roads are ancient salt routes along which caravans of merchants carried their precious cargo. In the Middle Ages, the lord and his family sat at a high table 'above the salt' – a fine piece of silverware – indicating their status. Those who were lower down the social scale sat 'below the salt'.

There are many customs associated with salt. The old proverb 'Help you to salt, help you to sorrow' means that it is bad luck to offer salt to a friend or a guest at a meal.

Knocking over a salt cellar is supposed to mean that a friendship will be broken.

It is also very bad luck to spill salt. Anyone who does so has to cancel out the bad luck by picking up a pinch of the spilt salt and throwing it over his or her left shoulder. No one is quite sure how this custom began. One theory is that people believed the evil spirits lurked behind the left shoulder. Throwing salt in their eyes blinded them and distracted them from evil deeds. In parts of Europe, people still sprinkle salt on the doorstep of a new house to ward off evil spirits.

•A Tea Ceremony in Japan•

To most of us, a cup of tea is a refreshing drink, quickly made by boiling a kettle and pouring hot water on to the tea-leaves or a tea-bag. Not so in Japan. There, drinking tea has a special significance. The whole business of making and serving the drink has to be carried out with a complex series of rituals.

Tea was introduced into Japan in the twelfth century, at about the same time as Zen Buddhism, which was to become one of the country's main religions. Buddhist monks took to drinking tea to keep themselves awake while they meditated for long periods. Then, the upper classes of society also began to drink tea as a fashionable way of passing the time.

Soon it became the custom to build special small houses where tea ceremonies were held for invited guests. The ceremonies included rituals for inducing peace and tranquillity of mind, in the tradition of Buddhist meditation.

Today, everybody in Japan drinks tea, but the ritual ceremony is still observed. The ceremony lasts four hours and every aspect is highly significant. People must wear the right clothes, eat the right foods, drink the right sort of tea and carry out the right sort of conversations. The result is a sort of meditation process which helps the participants to leave their everyday cares

THE CEREMONY

Guests change into special clothes before the ceremony begins. When they have looked at the implements which will be used to prepare the tea, they crawl through a low door, an action which gives them a feeling of humility towards each other. Then they take their seats.

The host prepares the charcoal and lights the fire, which the guests also examine. The host then serves food, but does not eat any. After a while, the 'koicha', or 'thick tea' is made, poured into small bowls and drunk by all the guests.

When everyone has drunk this tea, there is an interlude before the 'usucha', a less concentrated form of the same tea, is made and drunk.

Honey in Nepal

If a food is hard to find or collect, or if it has special properties which are not found in other foods, it is often highly valued. Honey has always been one such food. For thousands of years, people have taken great risks to collect it. Honey has medicinal value as well as being a natural sweetener and people will risk being stung by swarms of bees or falling to their deaths for it.

In some places in Nepal, men still make a perilous climb on rope ladders to reach honey lodged in otherwise inaccessible cliffs. The skills are passed from father to son, and only certain men who have the necessary know-how are allowed to take part.

A PERILOUS CLIMB
Starting at the top of the cliff, the man works his way slowly down the swinging rope ladder towards the bees' nest. Friends on a ledge above him hold the ladder steady. At the base of the cliff, other villagers light a fire to make smoke which calms the bees.

PREPARATION
Before setting out, the collector may bring himself luck by sprinkling rice grains in the air and reciting the names of the forest gods. He may also sacrifice a chicken and examine its insides to see if they contain any omens. These rituals are thought to protect the collector from being stung.

THE HARVEST
A pole is stuck into the outer part of the nest, known as the 'brood comb', which is rich in wax. As the wax is prised away, the collector levers the honeycomb into a basket on the end of another pole. The people at the bottom of the cliff hold pots and pans to catch any honey that spills. The honey will later be shared out, with most going to those who played the largest part in collecting it.

Giving and Sharing

Sharing food is a traditional way of cementing relationships between people, whether the occasion is an informal meal between friends, or a more formal gathering. The Wamira people of Papua New Guinea say that food must be shared with all who have set eyes on it, a custom which binds together the whole community. Giving food is another way of expressing feelings.

In many societies, it is customary to bring a gift of food or wine when invited to a meal at someone's house. This is a way of saying thank you and making a contribution to the proceedings. However, in Spain, Portugal and Italy, many hosts would be insulted if a guest brought wine.

Not all gifts are given in a spirit of kindness, however. A guest making a mistake would probably feel embarrassed. This feeling is played on by some societies. The Massim people of New Guinea embarrass people who have done wrong by heaping lavish gifts of food on them. It is the custom among the Massim that one gift must be returned by another, so the wrongdoer is showered with many more gifts than he can ever repay. He feels thoroughly embarrassed, and everyone else feels that they have had their revenge and shown him up in public.

BUTTER FESTIVAL, TIBET

In many Buddhist communities, there is a tradition that the people in the local community are responsible for providing food for the monks. In the Buddhist monasteries of Tibet, one of the highlights of the year was the butter festival, *which was held on the fifteenth day of the first moon. Sculptures of Tibetan bodhisattvas formed the centrepiece of the festival. These brightly coloured statues were made entirely from butter donated by wealthy patrons of the monastery.*

A BUTTER MOUNTAIN
The patrons donated huge quantities of butter made from yak's milk. The butter was mixed with powdered pigments in about twenty different colours.

COLD WORK
The monks worked hard for almost a month, moulding the figures. The work had to be done in cold rooms so that the butter did not melt. The monks had to keep dipping their fingers into cold water as they moulded the butter. It was hard and difficult work to create the spectacular statues.

Truffle Hunters

A truffle is a special type of fungus which is regarded as a great delicacy. Truffles are quite rare. Black and wrinkled, they grow underground, hard to find, and it has proved impossible to grow them to order. Combined with their distinctive flavour, this makes them expensive and sought-after luxuries.

Truffle-hunting is a familiar country pursuit in regions where the fungi grow. The Périgord region of southern France and parts of central Italy are some of the most well-known truffle-hunting areas. Most truffle-hunters find it too difficult to locate the elusive fungus without some outside help.

A dog to sniff them out is one solution, but the traditional partner of the truffle-hunter is a specially trained pig who roots about in the ground with its snout. The pigs are partial to the truffles they find, so the hunter often carries a stick to keep the pig away from any truffles it locates.

Some experts go truffle-hunting without any help. They use their personal experience and knowledge of where to look. A common place to find truffles is near the roots of trees, especially beech and oak, because they feed off the food that the tree makes.

Pig Festivals

In many communities, the possession of animals is seen as a status symbol. In most communities, it is better if the animals are alive, but not in Papua New Guinea. There the pig is seen as a symbol of wealth and power, and some tribes keep pigs as pets.

The pig festivals are a major part of life in Papua New Guinea. They are an occasion for friendly tribes to gather, and show their strength to potential enemies. The enemies are supposed to see what they are up against in terms of sheer numbers, and will think twice before attacking any tribe. Therefore the pig has an important role to play in keeping the peace among the tribes.

Pig festivals are only held about every ten years, because they take so long to organize. The organizing tribe begins by building new log houses for the guests to stay in. When the houses are ready, the invitations are sent out, the hosts begin to gather shells and money as gifts for their guests, and the pigs are fattened up, ready for their big day.

The hosts decorate their bodies with feathers and paint, and wait for the guests to arrive. When the guests have admired the pigs and the presents their hosts have provided, the pigs are slaughtered for the feast. About 200 pigs are killed, cut up and cooked in traditional earth ovens – deep pits filled with hot stones. When the meat is cooked, each male host divides it up among his family and guests. The best portions go to guests who have given the host pork at past festivals.

The guests take the pork home and share it out among their family and friends. They may hold a smaller festival to celebrate their friendship with the host tribe. Alliances have been renewed. The host tribe knows that the other tribes owe them a favour and that they realize that hosts who could lay on such a wonderful festival must be worth supporting.

Beer Festivals

B eer has been a popular drink for thousands of years in many different parts of the world. The ancient Egyptians enjoyed beer made from wheat and barley. There is a legend that Ra, the sun god, sent the cow-headed goddess, Hathor, to destroy the rebellious people on Earth. But the fearsome Hathor slew the people at such a rate that Ra regretted his action and poured beer over the Earth. The goddess lapped up the brew, collapsed in a stupor and the people escaped.

Clay tablets dating from 4000 BC show that the Babylonians knew how to make beer from barley and honey. By the time of the Roman Empire, beer was being made from hops, the usual ingredient today. The English, however, were reluctant to change to these newfangled ways and preferred to stick to their pre-Roman recipe, using herbs for flavouring. So began a distinction between the English ale, flavoured with herbs, and beer flavoured with hops. Ale became a drink for the poorer classes who could not afford wine, and by the ninth century, ale houses were a common sight in towns and villages.

But the flavour of hops appealed, and beer became a traditional drink in northern Europe. Hops grow well in the cool northern climate where vines are less easy to cultivate.

Beer-makers began to experiment with different brews, and national beers began to emerge. Dark brown bitter beers have become the traditional fare in British pubs, while pale lagers are popular in Germany, France and Scandinavia, and thick stout is a favourite brew in Ireland.

THE 'PLOUGHMAN'S LUNCH'

The plate of bread, cheese, pickles and salad served in British pubs conjures up the image of the trusty ploughman sitting under the hedge to unwrap his lunch after a hard morning's work. But nothing could be further from the truth. The 'ploughman's lunch', which has become a standard accompaniment to beer in most pubs, was invented by mid-twentieth-century pub owners looking for a cheap and easy-to-prepare meal.

Beer festivals began as a celebration of the hop harvest. They were joyous occasions for beer certainly added a sparkle to people's lives. A good harvest meant that there would be plenty of beer, and a profit for the brewers. Small beer, a much weaker brew, was drunk instead of water up to about 1820 in Europe.

Today, large beer festivals such as the Oktoberfest in Munich, Germany, and the Bockbier Festival in Berlin have gone far beyond the original festivities. They are carnival-like celebrations lasting for several days. Expert beer drinkers can sample different brews and give their verdicts, but everyone else is out to make merry, with dancing, music and singing. The beer is traditionally served in earthenware mugs, and white radishes are eaten to increase the thirst.

Wine Festivals

No one really knows why or when wine was first made but people have certainly been drinking it since about 4000 BC. One story is that wine was discovered at the court of King Jamshid, a ruler of ancient Persia. The king was fond of grapes and used to store them in a jar so that he could eat them whenever he pleased. But he he left one jar so long that the grapes began to rot and taste sour. The king thought they had become poisonous and so he labelled the jar 'Poison'.

One day, a lady in his harem decided to commit suicide by swallowing the poison. Little did she know that the grapes had in fact turned to wine which sent her into a deep sleep. When she woke up, she felt much more cheerful and went back to finish off the jar. And so, mythology says, wine was discovered!

Wine really came into its own with the rise of the Greek cultures. The Greeks enjoyed wine and took it with them to the countries they conquered. It was during this time that it found its way to Italy and France, which are now world-famous for their wine production.

THERE IS A *festival in Jerez in southern Spain every year to celebrate the latest batch of sherry to be released from the cellars where it has matured for over three years in ancient oak barrels.*

SOME OF THE *Chevaliers du Tastevin* preparing to taste the new vintages. A tastevin is a shallow silver dish with a handle on one side. Each Chevalier is presented with one when he or she is knighted; they wear them on a ribbon around their necks, so they are always ready to taste whatever is offered.

Wine makers rely on a good grape harvest to produce fine wine. If there is too much rain, the grapes will rot on the vine. If there is not enough sun, they do not ripen properly. When the harvest was good, people wanted to celebrate and they usually did this with a wine festival.

Wine festivals today take several forms. In some places, such as Barossa in Australia, there are grape treading competitions which go back to the time when the juice was squeezed out of the grapes by squashing them with bare feet. Competitors climb into large vats of grapes to see who can crush the most in the shortest time.

Other festivities are concerned with tasting the wines themselves. The most famous of these occasions is the wine auction at the Hospice de Beaune in Burgundy, France. The Hospice was founded in 1433 as a charity hospital for many beggars who lived in Beaune. It became the custom for wine growers in the region to give a part of the product of their vineyards to the Hospice so that the wine could be sold to raise money for the patients. The money raised at the auction still goes to the Hospice today.

The auction is held on the third Sunday in November and is the climax of a weekend of merry-making and wine drinking. On the day before the auction, hundreds of people gather to taste the wines. The wines are sold for very high prices but no one minds because the money is going to the Hospice.

A highlight of the weekend is a banquet given by the Confrerie de Chevaliers du Tastevin, the wine promoters of Burgundy. The banquet is held at their headquarters, the Chateau of the Clos du Vougeot. Five hundred Chevaliers process into the banqueting hall dressed in their official robes. They are followed by prospective new members of the fraternity who must be knighted with a vine branch before they can become fully-fledged Chevaliers. This weekend of non-stop revelry is the most famous wine event in the world.

Healing

Medicine today is very scientific, and there is little that is not known about the human body. Hospitals are equipped with modern machinery to monitor all manner of illnesses, and medicines are developed after much laboratory testing. Doctors and nurses are highly trained, and many diseases that used to be found throughout the world have been almost wiped out.

For thousands of years, people had no idea why a person became ill nor what to do about it. As early civilizations sought to explain the world around them, they looked to the gods for a solution. They reasoned that illness, like many other things, happened because the gods were displeased. So all manner of rituals were developed to appease the gods, including dancing, chanting and making offerings or sacrifices.

It was believed that certain people had powers to communicate with the spirits, heal the sick by laying their hands on them or devise a cure from natural ingredients such as herbs. These people became the healers, witch doctors or medicine men of their communities.

Traditional methods of healing still survive today, often operating side by side with the modern scientific approach. The traditional remedies described in this chapter are all very different, yet they have certain things in common. For one thing, they treat the whole person and not just the illness. The modern Western doctor discovers the patient's symptoms, diagnoses what is wrong and prescribes medicine for that complaint. Practitioners of alternative medicines, on the other hand, may pay attention to diet, the patient's state of mind and so on, as well as the illness itself.

Consulting Spirits

In many societies, the spirit world is the most important influence in life. If someone is ill, it is thought to have happened because people have behaved badly, and the spirits are angry. The first step towards healing is to communicate with the spirit who is causing the illness. The shaman is believed to have supernatural powers which allow him or her to do this. Because he or she is usually the only person in the community with such powers, the shaman is a revered member of society and may also assume the role of tribal leader or judge.

The shaman must try to get closer to the spirits, a process which he calls 'passing from one world to another'. To help him do this, he wears costumes that suggest mythical creatures or gods. For example, Japanese shamans wore hats made of owl and eagle feathers and cloaks decorated with stuffed snakes. Some shamans from the great plains of Siberia wear costumes that depict powerful animals such as bears and wild cats.

The shaman uses various rituals and ceremonies to communicate with the spirits, smooth their ruffled feelings and find out more about the disease he is treating. Many of the rituals involve music and dance, using words and movements that have been handed down for generations. Drumming is the most characteristic feature of these rituals. The beat of the drums establishes the rhythm of the dance and, many shamans say, opens up a path between the human and the spirit worlds.

The rituals that the shamans follow vary from place to place. For example, the Apache people of North America are afraid of coming into contact with the dead or even looking at dead bodies. The Apache believe that ghosts appear as owls, so they also dread catching sight of an owl. If someone becomes ill, the Apache may say it is because the person has seen an owl and is suffering from 'owl sickness' or 'ghost sickness'. The shaman is asked to come and sing over the person to discover more about the illness.

The Sioux people use song in a similar way. The writer Arthur Versluis described a modern example of healing by a shaman. A young boy was so ill that he could neither speak nor move. Conventional doctors had tried everything but failed to find a cure. Finally a Sioux shaman, Wallace Black Elk, was called. He came into the hospital room, shut the curtains so that it was completely dark and sang ritual songs. Black Elk later said that Tunkashila, a glowing figure representing God, appeared and told him that a spider's web had become lodged in his brain. The shaman summoned the red spider spirit who removed the web, and the boy was cured.

THE MASK OF THE SHAMAN

The shaman often wears a mask and costume to perform his healing rituals. This works in two ways. It helps the shaman to impersonate another being, which may be human or spiritual. It also disguises the shaman himself, which helps him when calling up the spirits. His own personality as a human being is obscured, making his passage to the spirit world more convincing.

TLINGIT MASK
The astonished expression on this Tlingit mask from the north-western American coast reminds watchers that the shaman's journey to the spirit world is dangerous.

The shaman has ritual objects to help him make contact with the spirit world. In southern Africa, for example, a shaman twirls a horse's mane to ward off evil spirits before beginning a healing ritual. Small objects such as shells, animals' teeth and beads are used to make a diagnosis. The shaman throws the objects into the air and makes a diagnosis according to the way they land. The position of the objects also helps the shaman to prescribe a suitable treatment such as herbal medicine or ritual bathing.

Another ritual is to send a spirit away from a sick person. In north-western Australia, the shaman sucks the spirit out of the patient's body, carries it away in his hands and buries it. A ritual once common in Africa involved transferring the spirit to an animal which was then killed, so curing the disease.

Training Rituals

It is not enough simply to have the power or to inherit the role of shaman. Before becoming a healer, a would-be shaman must go through a long training which begins when young.

First, they must show that they have the mental stamina to cope with the spirit world. They spend long periods living alone, cut off from other people. They must fast and remain silent for days on end. This should put them into the right frame of mind for communicating with the spirits.

The training also covers aspects of their healing powers. They must call up a spirit vision which shows them some of the rituals they will carry out in the future. Among the Yakut people of Siberia, the trainee shaman is handed over to evil spirits who tear his body to pieces and eat parts of it. The parts eaten by the spirits tell the shaman what his powers will be. If the spirits eat his stomach, he will be able to cure stomach illnesses, and so on.

THIS SIBERIAN SHAMAN'S *costume conceals the whole body. The shaman is disguised behind a host of symbols, including images of the spirits, a mirror to help him see into the other world, and ribbons called 'wings' that indicate the ability to fly.*

The young shaman is taught by a fully trained healer who instructs him in the use of medicinal plants, tells him about the ceremonies and dances he will have to perform and the music he will use. In some parts of South America, the shaman learns how to perform acts which seem like magic. Working in a haze of tobacco smoke, he is able to take objects such as stones and insects from the diseased parts of people's bodies.

The power of the shamans is enormous, even though some of their methods look like elaborate tricks. They can cure people because they believe in them. All forms of medicine rely to some extent on this psychological approach.

•The Power of Touch•

Healers from very different traditions use the power of touch, or the laying-on of hands. It is as though a health-giving power is passed through the fingers to the patient. In some cases, there is a scientific explanation for the success of the method. But others are a mystery which seems to be linked more closely to the spirit world than to the world of science.

HOLISTIC MASSAGE
The term 'holistic' means that the treatment covers the whole body, not just the diseased or injured part. The masseur first massages individual parts of the body, and then makes long 'connecting' strokes to join all the parts of the treatment together.

REFLEXOLOGY
Reflexologists work only on the feet, but the treatment is regarded as being holistic because the pressure points on the feet are said to affect the energy flow to all parts of the body (see page 66).

CHRISTIAN FAITH-HEALER
The laying-on of hands in Christian faith-healing rituals goes back to the work of Jesus himself, who healed the sick by placing his hands on them. Some Christian ministers still hold healing services in which prayer is combined with healing rites such as the laying-on of hands. For the treatment to work, the sick person must have faith and believe that healing power is coming through the healer's fingers into his or her own body.

WORKING ON THE AURA
Some healers treat disease by working on the person's 'aura', the invisible ring that surrounds the body. These healers never actually touch the patient's body.

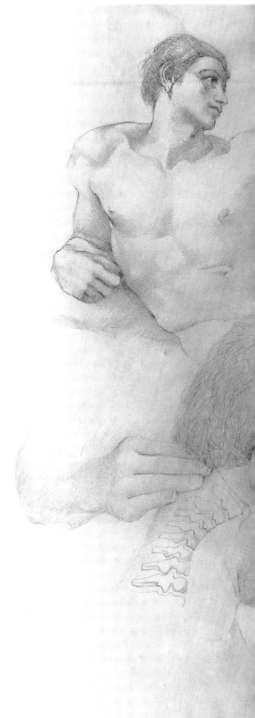

OSTEOPATHY

An osteopath manipulates and re-aligns the bones of the body to ease muscular pain such as backache. Osteopaths have a detailed knowledge of the skeleton and muscles, and know how the various nerves are affected by joints which are out of line. He or she will locate a place where the bones are 'out of joint' and,

after some gentle manipulation and massage to relax the muscles around the joint, will give a sudden sharp manipulation to click the bones back into place. The osteopath must also continually check the alignment of the bones in the skeleton, making as many adjustments as are necessary to ease pressure on the nerves which are causing pain.

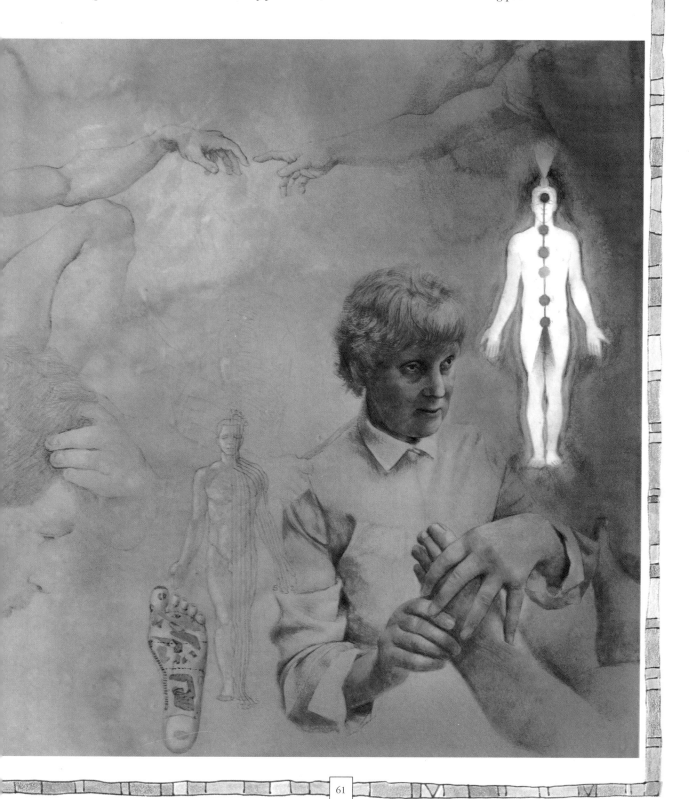

FIGWORT

The Latin name for this plant, Scrophularia nodosa, tells us that it was once used in the treatment of scrofula, a form of tuberculosis which was caused by drinking contaminated milk. This disease, which caused painful abscesses in the neck, is now quite rare. Today, figwort is more likely to be used in the treatment of skin diseases.

PASQUE FLOWER

The English name for Anemone pulsatilla, comes from an old French word for Easter, because this plant was traditionally gathered at Easter when it was in flower. The stems of the herb were used for disorders of the reproductive system.

GINGER

Ginger (Zingiber officinale) is most well-known as a spice used in cooking, but it is also used in medicines by both Western and Chinese herbalists. In the West, it is used to relieve indigestion, and herbalists from both traditions use it to treat colds and flu. However, they distinguish between fresh ginger, which is used for colds, and dry ginger, used for respiratory and digestive problems.

MOTHERWORT

This plant was traditionally given to women after childbirth, as its name suggests. The Latin name, Leonurus cardiaca, tells us that it was used to treat palpitations, a condition that makes the heart beat rapidly and with greater force than usual.

EYEBRIGHT

A traditional English remedy, eyebright (Euphrasia officinalis) is best-known as a remedy for diseases of the eye. It is also used to treat sinusitis and nasal catarrh.

COMFREY

The roots and leaves of comfrey (Symphytum officinale) are used by herbalists to treat a wide range of disorders, including gastric ulcers and coughs. Comfrey also helps wounds to heal more quickly.

Healing Plants

As people began to learn more about plants thousands of years ago, they discovered that some herbs have medicinal properties. These discoveries were probably made by accident, but as time went by, people experimented with herbs, mixing them with other ingredients to make the first medicines. For thousands of years, no other types of medicines were available.

The first potions were probably of a cure-all variety, but people gradually learned how to make medicines for specific ailments. The first herbalists were people who had studied the local plants and learned what each could do. They gave each plant a name such as 'self-heal', 'woundwort' or 'eyebright' to remind themselves of its medicinal uses. The common names of many plants still reflect their traditional uses.

White Witches

Early herbalists, who were mainly women, built up a vast store of knowledge which was passed down through the generations. People who were ill went to these 'wise women', who would diagnose the complaint and mix up a brew to cure it.

Later, herbalists devised another way of prescribing plants, which was that like always cured like. In other words, a plant that resembled a disease would cure it. If a plant had kidney-shaped leaves, for example, it was said to help disorders of the kidneys.

Customs developed about the time when the plants should be harvested. There were often practical reasons for these rules. Roots were always gathered at the end of the growing season, for example, because that is when they contain the most nutrients. The wise women were only using what nature had to offer, but when they worked the cures seemed like magic, so many people viewed the herbalists with suspicion. During the Middle Ages churchmen branded these women as witches. They risked persecution and even death for their healing powers.

These 'white witches' were different from the wicked witches of storybooks who practised black magic, but any type of witch was thought to have powers beyond those of other people, and was an unpopular figure. Different countries had their own rituals for getting rid of them. In some villages in southern Italy, March was supposed to be the month when witches were at large, and so a ritual for expelling them was carried out every Friday evening in March. The church bells pealed out, and people ran through the streets, crying out, 'March is come'.

Walpurgis Night on the eve of May Day was the time for expelling witches in Central Europe. The ritual was known as 'Burning out the Witches'. After the evening church bells had rung, men and boys rang bells and banged pots and pans together. Dogs were let loose to run through the streets, barking and yelping. Then, bundles of twigs from plants such as rosemary and sloe were attached to poles and set alight. All the bells in the village were rung, and people shouted at the same time, 'Witch flee, flee from here, or it will go ill with thee.' Then, still carrying the burning twigs, the people ran around the village seven times, to smoke the witches out of their lairs.

Oriental Medicine

Doctors who practise Chinese medicine believe that it is important to balance the two opposite forces in the body, the 'yin', or negative influences, and 'yang' or positive influences. The origins of this approach date back to a ruler of China, Shen Nung, who was inspired by a Taoist leader called Ban Gu. It was believed that the two opposites combined with the blood and flowed around the body. If the opposites were not perfectly balanced, a person became ill. If the flow stopped altogether, the person died.

Diet is an important part of this philosophy. The Chinese believe that some foods are yin and others are yang, and that people must eat the right balance of both types. This dietary system is known as 'macrobiotics'. Foods are classified according to the nutrients they contain, where they are grown, and their colour, texture and taste. Wholegrains form a large part of the macrobiotic diet.

Herbs also play an important part in Oriental medicine. Chinese herbalists make up medicines from a vast selection of plants, many of which have been used for thousands of years. Many of these herbs are also used in cooking, which ties in well with the Chinese ideas about the importance of diet. Herbs are included in food to keep the yin and yang balance constant, as well as for flavour. Food and medicine work together to promote good health.

There used to be a tradition in China that people saw the doctor on a regular basis, not just when they were ill. The doctor made sure that people were maintaining their yin and yang balance and staying healthy. People only paid the doctor when they were well. If they fell ill, they stopped paying until their yin and yang balance was back to normal.

Another method of restoring the balance of the body is acupuncture, a Chinese practice which is now used world-wide.

Traditional Chinese medicine holds that the life-force, or 'chi', flows through the body along channels called 'meridians'. A blockage in one of these meridians prevents the effective flow of chi and causes ill health. The acupuncturist inserts needles into the patient's skin at various points on the affected meridian to get the chi flowing properly and restore the balance of the body. Acupuncture charts show the points and the meridians they lie on. Acupuncturists learn which points affect the various parts of the body.

THE BELIEF IN *'yin' and 'yang' underpins all Chinese beliefs. This says that everything has two separate and opposing elements which together make up a whole. Yin is negative, dark and female; Yang is positive, bright and male.*

Diagnosis of the patient's complaint has to be very accurate, so that the acupuncturist knows which points to use. In Chinese medicine, diagnosis is made by examining the patient's twelve pulses – there are six in each wrist. Each pulse is believed to give information about a particular part of the body. The needles, which range from 2.5 to 25 centimetres long, are inserted painlessly and left in position, sometimes for several hours.

Acupuncture can be used as a pain-killing treatment or an anaesthetic for major operations, as well as to cure specific complaints. In the West, it is sometimes used in conjunction with orthodox medicine, as an additional treatment. Chinese doctors still prefer to use acupuncture, herbal medicines and other traditional methods for common illnesses rather than modern drugs.

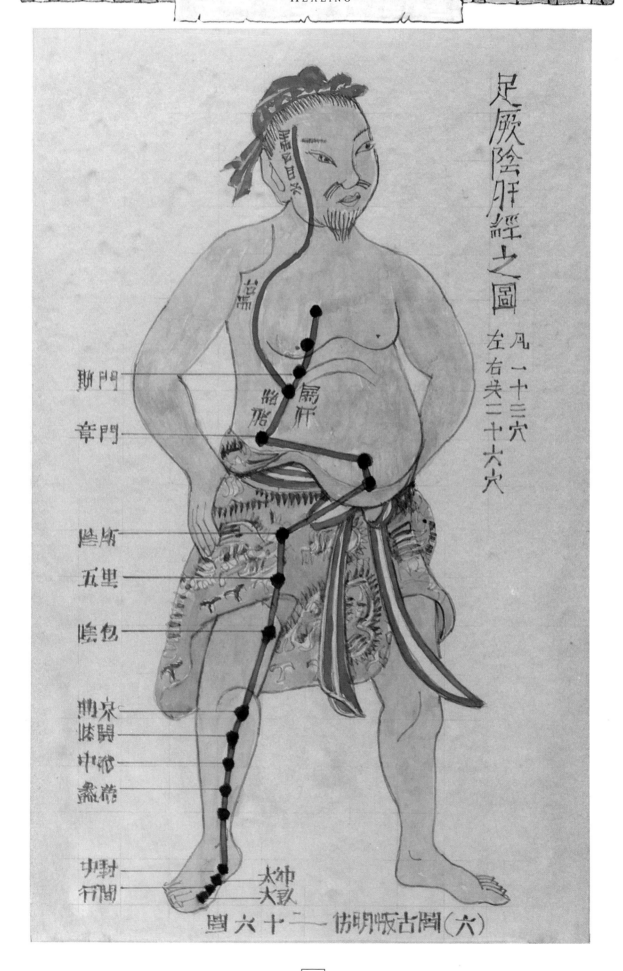

•Alternative Medicine•

Alternative medicine is the name given to any medical system which is not based on the science taught in medical schools. Not all of these systems are based on ancient traditions like herbal medicine and acupuncture. People relied on these old methods for centuries, but during the late eighteenth and early nineteenth centuries, several new techniques were introduced, including 'chiropractic', 'homeopathy' and 'naturopathy'.

The popularity of alternative medicine declined during the early part of the twentieth century, however, because many new discoveries had been made in the field of orthodox medicine. Vaccines, antibiotics and improved techniques in surgery meant that doctors were using what were considered more 'scientific' methods to cure patients. In recent years, some people have swung back to alternative methods because of their holistic approach. People began to question whether it was a good thing to swallow pills for any complaint, without necessarily finding the deep-rooted cause of the illness.

As a result of this approach, new and rediscovered methods began to emerge, such as 'reflexology' and 'aromatherapy'. Some people will only use the alternative methods, while others combine orthodox medicine with some of the alternatives. For example, they would go to hospital to have their appendix taken out, but they might go to an osteopath with back pain or an aromatherapist for stress-related complaints.

Chiropractic is based on the theory that disease is caused, at least in part, by nerves not functioning properly and so sending incorrect signals to the brain. Chiropractors treat various illnesses by manipulating the spine to relieve pressure on nerves.

Homeopathy was developed by a German physician, Samuel Hahnemann, at the end of the eighteenth century. His revolutionary new method caused such controversy among

BORN IN GERMANY *in 1755, Samuel Hahnemann studied medicine at Leipzig and Vienna. He was dissatisfied with the medicine he learned and looked for a new and more effective way of treating illnesses.*

fellow doctors that Hahnemann had to leave his practice in Leipzig, and finally settled in Paris. The principle of homeopathy is based on the principle that 'like cures like'. To treat an illness, a homeopath gives the patient very tiny doses of a drug that, in larger doses, would bring on symptoms of the disease in a healthy person. The drugs used seemed very controversial to many people, including such things as arsenic and snake venom as well as herbs and other natural substances. Arsenic is a strong poison, but very tiny amounts are present in water and some foods, so most people have minute quantities in their bodies.

Homeopathy has quite a large following around the world today.

Naturopathy is based on the principle that disease is due to poisonous substances building up in the body, mainly because of poor diet and environmental pollution. Patients visiting a naturopath would be put on a diet containing no artificial additives or refined foods. The diet would also include foods containing nutrients that are especially beneficial for the particular complaint.

Acupressure is similar to acupuncture, except that pressure is applied to the points instead of needles. Reflexology is another system in which particular points are said to influence the whole body. In this case, the practitioner massages different parts of the patient's feet to cure disorders in other parts.

Aromatherapy is a range of treatments using aromatic oils taken from plants such as lavender. Many ancient civilizations, including the Chinese, used such 'essential oils' to treat various disorders. Aromatherapy is particularly good for disorders brought on by stress, because the treatment itself is relaxing. The oil is massaged into the body, or inhaled. It can also be put into bath water or incorporated into creams and lotions.

·Driving Out Evil Spirits·

In some traditional societies, people believe that disasters and illnesses are caused by evil spirits which have to be driven out. There are many different techniques for this. On the Indonesian island of Nias, if someone was seriously ill and other remedies had failed, it would be assumed that the devil was causing the illness, and a sorcerer would be called to exorcize it.

A pole was set up outside the patient's house, and a palm-leaf rope was stretched from the top of the pole to the roof of the house. The sorcerer climbed on to the roof carrying a pig which he then killed and rolled down the roof to the ground. The idea was that the devil would be so anxious to get the pig that he would leave the house and slide down the rope of palm leaves. The sorcerer then called on a good spirit to stop the devil climbing up again.

If the person was not cured by this particular ritual, it was assumed that there must be more than one devil in the house. Now everyone became involved in finding the devils and driving them out. All the doors and windows were closed except for one window in the roof. The men went through

ON NIAS, THE *sorcerer has climbed the ladder on to the roof of his patient's hut and is about to kill the pig to tempt out the devil causing the illness.*

the house, chopping and slashing at the air with swords. Other people banged on gongs and drums. The theory was that all this pandemonium would terrify the devils so much that they would rush to escape through the open window.

If there was an epidemic of some illness among the people of Ghana in West Africa, everyone would turn out to drive away the evil spirits. They carried clubs and torches which they waved as they ran in and out of houses and up and down the streets, shouting as loudly as they could. When they believed that the spirits had been driven out of the village, they chased after them into the forests, shouting that they must never return. When the spirits had been banished, all the cocks in the village were killed in case their crowing showed the spirits the way back.

On the island of Sulawesi in Indonesia, if

demons were causing illness or disaster, the people moved out of their houses into huts just outside the village. The demons were left to their own devices in the deserted village. The villagers spent several days in the huts, offering sacrifices and preparing for the exorcism itself.

When the time came, the men put on masks or blackened their faces, armed themselves with swords, guns or broomsticks, and crept silently back to the village. They waited in silence until the priest gave the signal. Then they broke into furious yelling, and charged into the village, striking at doors, windows and walls to chase the devils out. The priest and the other villagers followed them, carrying the holy fire, and marched around each house nine times. The holy fire then had to burn in the kitchen for three days without going out.

Gift-giving

Giving and receiving gifts is a ritual carried out by people from almost all societies. Gifts are exchanged for several reasons. They can mark anniversaries such as birthdays or religious festivals like Christmas. They can be given as a mark of respect, a token of thanks, or as a celebration of an event such as a marriage or the birth of a baby. The gifts themselves can be lavish and expensive, or things of mainly symbolic value, such as cards.

Why do we give gifts? They are a way of showing people how we feel about them or that we are thinking of them at a particular time. We also establish a special type of relationship with the people we give gifts to. Often, we are expected to exchange gifts. If someone gives you a present on your birthday, it is customary to give a birthday present in return.

Some people worry about the value of the gift as well. Was the present they bought less valuable than the one they got in return, for example? Manufacturers have cashed in on this idea, packaging up goods at times like Christmas and Easter to make them look more luxurious and cost twice the price.

The custom of taking a 'house-warming' present to someone who has just moved into a new house has its origins in ancient superstition. People once believed that as soon as a house had been built, spirits moved in along with the new occupiers. The gifts were supposed to keep the spirits happy.

ACCORDING TO THE *Gospel of St Luke*, *the three wise men offered the baby Jesus gold in token of his kingship, frankincense in token of his godhead, and myrrh which was a rare and valuable spice used for embalming the dead.*

One of the big gift-giving occasions of the year is the Christian festival of Christmas. The tradition began with gifts brought to the infant Christ by the 'Magi', or 'Three Wise Men'. Young children associate the gifts they get at Christmas with Santa Claus, also known as Father Christmas.

Santa Claus is derived from the name of St Nicholas, the patron saint of Christmas. The tradition that he comes down the chimney and fills children's stockings with presents began with a legend. St Nicholas, who was actually the Bishop of Myra in about AD 300, went to the home of three sisters who were very poor and threw some coins down the chimney. The coins fell into some stockings which the sisters had left hanging by the fire to dry. When they woke up the next morning, the sisters were overjoyed to find money in their stockings.

Ever since, children have hung up stockings in the hope that Santa Claus will come down the chimney and fill them. In the Netherlands, St Nicholas visits each house on his feast, 6 December, to check up on the children's behaviour before leaving his presents for those judged to have been good.

Today, the giving of gifts at Christmas outweighs the religious aspect of the festival in many people's minds. The shops begin to stock up with cards, gifts and decorations months beforehand, and children prepare their lists of requests and write letters to Santa Claus. People send cards to friends they may never see during the rest of the year. In houses everywhere, presents are carefully wrapped in Christmas paper and hidden away or put around the Christmas tree. They must not be opened until Christmas morning!

Potlatch Celebrations

When the Spanish and English explorers arrived on the north-west coast of America in the eighteenth century, they were astonished to find wealthy communities living in large wooden houses and villages filled with elaborately carved columns and posts, showing animals and mythical beings. They realized that they were among people who valued wealth and possessions highly. This was reflected in a lavish ceremony of feasting and gift giving known as 'potlatch', a word that means 'giving'. The most elaborate potlatch ceremonies were held during the nineteenth century, but the Kwakiuti people still have them today.

Potlatches were traditionally held to celebrate some particular event such as a birth or a peace agreement between separate groups. They were laid on by the tribal chiefs as a way of showing their leadership and keeping the people loyal to them. The ceremony had to be carried out with elaborate ritual. Invited guests arrived dressed in ceremonial clothes. The host waited for them in his house, with his family crowded around in the big room, a blazing fire burning in the central hearth.

As each guest arrived, the host greeted them and showed them where to sit. He introduced them to his wife and family, and made a speech in honour of his dead father who had been the chief before him. Then, he displayed the gifts he was about to give them, which were often lavish. There would be blankets, oil, copper shields and trays, weapons, war clothing and even canoes.

It is said that at one ceremony in the early twentieth century, about 33,000 blankets were given. Then, masked dancers performed in honour of the host and his ancestors. The potlatch went on far into the night, each stage following tradition and ritual.

POTLATCH, NORTH-WEST AMERICA

The Kwakiuti people still carry out their traditional potlatch ceremony, a large tribal gathering at which the host entertains guests to a lavish feast and distributes gifts. By holding such a ceremony, the host confirms his position as the chief of the people by giving them hospitality and gifts which they could never hope to repay. The ceremony was banned in 1884, but illegal potlatches continued. The law banning them was repealed in 1951.

ARRIVAL OF THE GUESTS

Invited guests arrive in their brightly painted canoes for the potlatch ceremony. In the background are totem poles. At the ceremony, the guests are seated according to a complicated protocol system, and all the events such as speech-making and feasting follow in a certain order which never varies. The climax of the ceremony is the handing out of the gifts. Blankets used to be the traditional gift, but nowadays various gifts such as money and clothes are given.

·Kula in the Trobriand Islands·

The people of the Trobriand Islands in the south-western Pacific Ocean have a traditional form of exchange called the 'kula', in which gifts continually circulate around the island group. The gifts are passed from person to person and from island to island in a continuous exchange. Two types of gifts are exchanged in the kula. Long necklaces made from red shells are passed in a clockwise direction around the islands, and bracelets of white shells move in the opposite direction. Each person taking part in the kula keeps an item for a short time before passing it on to the next person.

THE BENEFITS OF EXCHANGE

The ritual of kula gives the Trobriand islanders the opportunity of meeting people from other islands. It is also a way of keeping the tribes on the different islands friendly with one another. The need to travel between the islands encourages the people to build sea-going canoes and set up trading links.

THE RITUALS OF EXCHANGE

Only the male islanders take part in the kula. The men who are carrying out a particular exchange board a sea-going canoe and set sail for the next island. The men have with them the necklaces or bracelets which they are going to exchange.

When they arrive at the next island, there is a ceremony in which they offer a necklace to the chief of the island's tribe. The necklace will have travelled a long distance by then and will have a long ritual history. The men who are presenting it may explain its history, telling who has held it and on which islands.

The islanders may also carry out more conventional trading at the same time as the ritual exchange.

· Forced Gifts and Feasts ·

Many of the ancient civilizations had a form of gift-giving known as 'tribute'. This was the presentation of goods by loyal subjects to their ruler, often because they were forced into it. The Aztecs of Mexico exacted tribute from all the peoples in their mighty empire.

The emperor and nobility living in the city of Tenochtitlan built up great wealth and a magnificent lifestyle by taking a constant stream of goods from their subjects, including exotic foods, feathers, cloaks, armour, weapons, precious stones and metals. When the Aztecs conquered a new city-state, a tribute list – of all the things the city had to pay to the Aztecs – was produced at once.

There are many other examples of tribute. The peoples of the Persian Empire brought magnificent gifts to the king's palace at Persepolis (in Iran).

Carvings show queues of people, Bactrians bringing camels, Medes with horses, Ethiopians with elephant tusks, and other peoples with rich cloth or jewellery.

The tradition of tribute still continues – in Ethiopia, peasants pay tribute in return for their land. In other parts of Africa, people pay tribute to local chiefs in return for hospitality in the form of public feasts and protection in times of trouble. In some ways, the system is similar to the taxes which people pay to governments for services.

IN THE SOLOMON *Islands of the Pacific, a free feast was a traditional way of giving. The host would be someone who hoped to become a leader or 'big man', and wanted to get the better of a rival for the role.*

The host presented his rival with hundreds of pigs and large amounts of shell money. The aim was to show what a generous man the host was, and shame the rival into admitting that he could not return gifts of equal value. The food for the feast was displayed in a specially built wooden tower. Everyone could marvel at the host's generosity.

The rivals could often go on for years trying to match each other's lavish feasts until one of them failed to do so and the other was declared the winner.

Helping the Poor

Giving gifts has been a part of religion since the earliest civilizations. First came the idea of making offerings to the gods in order to please them. From this stemmed the idea of giving food and money to the priests who were acting on behalf of the gods.

In ancient Egypt, people gave money to the priests to make offerings of food at the temples. Food would be left at the temples. When the gods did not appear to take the food, the priests ate it, on the understanding that they were doing it on behalf of the gods.

In medieval Europe, people gave a 'tithe', or one-tenth of their income, to the Church as support for the clergy. This custom developed from the laws set out in the Jewish Torah which said that the 'first fruits' of the season should be given as an offering to God. So Jews had to give payment in the form of agricultural produce. The Christian Church adopted this idea to help maintain its churches and priests. Later, money was given instead of produce. Tithes were paid in Britain up to 1936, when the law was abolished, and some people still pay them voluntarily. Buddhist monks are also supported by the local people who give money, or 'alms', to buy them food.

Religious teaching also encourages people who have money to give to those who have not. Muslims pay a special tax which is used for charitable purposes. When a baby is born to a Muslim family, it is customary for them to give money to the poor.

Christians are also encouraged to give to charities which support needy people. Giving to others can do the giver some good by making him look generous in other people's eyes, and making a show of giving has always been frowned upon. In his Sermon on the Mount, Christ said that people should give alms discreetly so that others did not know where they came from.

WHEN PEOPLE GIVE *food to a Buddhist monk, they not only help him to survive but also benefit themselves. Buddhists believe that the good deeds they perform, such as giving to the monks, will be acknowledged during this lifetime, or in a later life.*

A Part of Your Soul?

People often give each other photographs of themselves as a keepsake. Photos of family members are put on display, and some people carry pictures of loved ones around with them. But in some parts of the world, people hate having their photo taken because they believe it will bring them bad luck.

This superstition comes from an ancient idea that the face is a reflection of the soul. Taking a photograph of someone therefore takes part of the soul away from that person. If the photograph is then given to someone else, that person is said to have power over the person in the photograph, and may use it to harm them.

Some people also think that it is bad luck to tear up a photograph of someone who is alive, because the action may harm that person. If a portrait or photograph of a

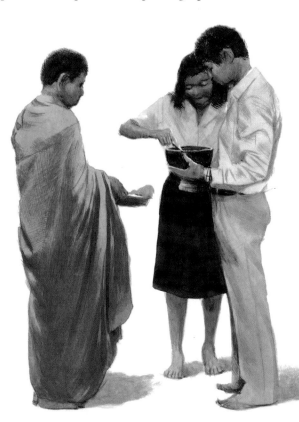

person falls off a wall or down from a shelf for no apparent reason, this is seen as a very bad omen and the subject of the picture is likely to die soon afterwards.

These ideas may come from the many ancient superstitions surrounding mirrors. People used to believe that the reflection seen in a mirror was the person's soul, which led to the many superstitions surrounding the breaking of mirrors. If a mirror was broken, the reflection would be shattered, and so the soul was destroyed and the person would die soon afterwards. Although people are not usually so terrified of breaking mirrors today, many still believe that it may bring seven years' bad luck.

However, there is an old English custom for warding off the bad luck caused by breaking a mirror. All the pieces must be collected up and thrown into a fast flowing river or stream so that the bad luck is swept away by the water.

•Mother's Day•

In some countries, certain days have been set aside for giving gifts to particular members of the family. Some of these, such as Father's Day, are geared to the manufacturers of cards and presents as much as anything else. But 'Mothering Sunday' or 'Mother's Day', which falls on the second Sunday in March, dates back to a medieval Christian tradition. Nowadays, Mothering Sunday is the time when sons and daughters buy a special card or present for their mothers. At church services held on this day, young children are given posies of flowers to present to their mothers, as a special 'thank you'.

The tradition of Mothering Sunday dates back to the time when Lent, the period of fasting leading up to Easter, was very strictly observed. Lent lasts for forty days, beginning on Ash Wednesday, in recognition of the forty days Christ spent in the wilderness. In the Middle Ages, people were not allowed to eat any meat during Lent and generally fasted very strictly.

People found the strain of the fast so rigorous that in 1216, Pope Innocent III introduced a religious festival called 'Golden Rose' or 'Laetare' (Rejoice) Sunday on the fourth Sunday. This was the one day during Lent when people could relax their fast and enjoy themselves. In England, Golden Rose Sunday became the day when young people working as apprentices and maids could go home, visit their 'Mother Church' and see their parents. So the day gradually came to be known as Mothering Sunday.

When the young people arrived home, they would find that their mother had prepared a special celebration meal, which was usually roast lamb followed by 'frumenty', a traditional dish made from grains of wheat boiled in milk with sugar and spices. Another traditional dish was 'carlings', pancakes made from peas and fried in butter.

And so the mother who prepared this delicious meal during a time of such austerity gradually became the central figure of Golden Rose Sunday. On the way home through the country lanes, the young people would pick bunches of wild flowers to give to their mothers to say 'thank you'. By now, it had become the tradition for people to go home to visit their mothers rather than their Mother Church.

The custom lasted for centuries, but by the end of Queen Victoria's reign at the end of the nineteenth century, it had begun to die out. It was the Americans who revived it

during World War II by bringing their own Mother's Day customs to England.

Today, Mother's Day in America is celebrated on the second Sunday in May. On that day, sons and daughters wear a white carnation if their mother is dead and a red one if she is still alive. Other countries also celebrate Mothering Sunday. French children give their mothers flowers on the last Sunday in May, for example.

IN 1914, PRESIDENT *Woodrow Wilson had set aside 9 May as a special day for mothers in the USA after being persuaded by the campaigning of a Miss Anna Jarvis from Philadelphia.*

Miss Jarvis, whose own mother had died on 9 May 1905, reasoned that everyone has a mother and so a special day for mothers was one which every family could celebrate.

Settling Disputes

People cannot always be in agreement with one another, nor is it always easy to decide who is right in an argument. Tempers may become heated and people become hot-headed, and arguments between two or more people can escalate into full-scale warfare. So all societies have developed ways of sorting out people's differences, and helping them to reach agreement.

 **W**ays of settling a dispute vary a great deal from society to society. Methods range from leaving the people to fight it out between themselves, to court-room trials in which the verdict is decided by a judge and jury. Some societies have unusual ways of settling matters, such as the Inuit custom of singing insults to an opponent.

Fist-fighting is the most basic way of sorting out a disagreement. This can range from an unofficial punch-up to formal fights with rules and regulations. In medieval England, knights would joust with each other to win a lady's hand. Duelling with swords or pistols was another way to settle a disagreement between gentlemen.

Some disputes arise on the spur of the moment. Others are deeply plotted methods of revenge. Feuds between families or tribes can last for years, seeking revenge for some slight. A feud normally started because a member of one family killed a member of another. Understandably, the family of the dead person were not too pleased about this, but instead of killing the killer, they killed someone else in the family. The other family retaliated and so the feud continued.

Trial by Jury

Since ancient times, societies have found that the fairest way to settle disputes is for a third party, such as a judge, to listen to both sides of an argument and decide who is right.

In order to make fair judgements, societies drew up laws to tell people what they could and could not do, and the penalties for disobedience. One of the most famous set of laws of the ancient world was put together by King Hammurabi of Babylon in about 1770 BC. The 282 laws, which were engraved on huge stone tablets and set up across his kingdom, worked on the principle of 'an eye for an eye, a tooth for a tooth'. A son who struck his father could expect to have his hands chopped off, while a person who blinded someone had his eyes gouged out.

The Incas of Peru did not take crime lightly either. Any commoner committing a crime against the state or members of the nobility risked having his brains beaten out with a club or being hanged upside-down until he was dead.

The Vikings settled disputes at a special open-air meeting called a 'Thing'. Family feuds which got out of hand were often taken

to the Thing to be resolved. Each region of the Viking territories had its own set of laws which were used to decide on a verdict at these meetings.

The courts in modern industrialized societies follow rituals which are steeped in tradition. The special gowns and wigs worn by judges and lawyers, the legal language and the titles by which members of the court refer to one another, such as 'your honour' and 'm'lud' in British courts, seem very old-fashioned and a little pompous. But observing strict traditions in this way has various advantages. It makes the court seem more distant from everyday life, and therefore inspire respect and perhaps fear in the people involved. The traditions make the proceedings more formal, and by presenting the judges and lawyers in their official costumes, make it less likely that people will bear personal grudges for a judgement which they do not agree with.

·Trial by Ordeal or Combat··

Trials by ordeal or combat are similar ways of sorting out differences because each person or group accepts a challenge from the other. The most extreme trial by combat is an all-out war. Both sides will fight until one side wins or a solution for peace can be found.

During the Middle Ages in Europe, the most glorious honour a man could hope for was to become a knight, riding into battle in shining armour, his horse decked in splendid livery. The life of a knight was ruled entirely by fighting to maintain his honour. To the medieval knight, death was better than dishonour, and many were killed jousting in tournaments. The knights fought with a lance while on horseback, and also carried a broadsword or mace to fight with should they be unhorsed and have to fight on the ground.

Sometimes the tournaments were laid on as entertainment for the spectators, but combats to the death were also organized by warring parties, over a power struggle or some point of honour. Two nobles might appoint knights to fight the battle for them.

Medieval Christians believed that God would favour the side which had been wronged, and so that knight would win. The term 'throwing down the gauntlet' comes from the custom of throwing down a gauntlet or mailed glove as a challenge to fight.

Until fairly recent times, arguments between two men could lead to a challenge to a duel. Each man would appoint someone to be his 'second' and see fair play. Early duels were fought with swords, later ones with pistols. For a pistol duel, the procedure was for each man to walk a given number of paces away from one another, turn and fire. Men in America used a similar method of sorting out

their differences during the days of the Wild West. The quickest on the draw won the day.

Duels are still fought in some societies. Wrestling is the traditional way of resolving disputes among the Inuit of Alaska, Baffinland and Siberia, while the tribes who live along the Arctic Circle from Hudson Bay to the Bering Straits use a type of struggle called 'buffeting'. The opponents stand facing each other and hit out with straight-armed blows to the side of the head. When one of the duellers has been knocked out, the other one is declared the winner. The winner goes up in everyone's estimation, while the loser suffers severe loss of face.

TRIAL BY ORDEAL

In a trial of ordeal, the two warring parties have to endure some ordeal, and the one who suffers the least is declared the winner. The ordeal may be to walk across a fire or plunge a hand into boiling water.

People who carry out this type of trial believe that the gods or spirits will help the innocent party and make sure that the guilty one is injured. In the same way, the medieval Christians believed that God would help the innocent party in combat. If someone refuses to accept a challenge, this is taken as a sign of guilt.

THE PHILIPPINES
The Ifugao people of the Philippines judge criminal cases and property disputes by subjecting the accused parties to ordeals. A popular method is the hot-water ordeal, in which each of the parties must plunge a hand into a pot of boiling water, pull out a pebble, and then put the pebble back in the water. The person who is less badly burned or scalded is judged to be the innocent party or the one who is in the right.

THE SOLOMON ISLANDS
The Kwaio of the Solomon Islands bring the spirits of their ancestors into their trials by ordeal. Even a guilty person may pray to an ancestor for help. If someone says they are not guilty when they are, survives the ordeal unscathed or is let off anyway, this is seen as an ancestor intervening to help out.

Artistic Contests

The Inuit people of Greenland duel by head-butting, but they also introduce another aspect into settling disputes. This is the song-duel, a contest in which the opponents use traditional and specially composed songs to heap insults on each other. A song-duel can last for months or even years, though most are over much more quickly than this. This example is a song to a man who has stolen his opponent's wife:

An impudent, black-skinned oaf has stolen her,
Has tried to belittle her.
A miserable wretch who loves human flesh,
A cannibal from famine days.

When the opponents have run out of insults to hurl at each other, the spectators make a judgement in favour of one or the other. There is no punishment for the person who is found to be in the wrong. Everyone simply heaves a sigh of relief that each side has had its say and the conflict is over. The two parties now go back to living normal lives and often remain the best of friends, once they have got their grievances off their chests. The duel has taken the heat out of the quarrel and has also provided great entertainment for the rest of the community.

In some communities, people air their grievances with an artistic performance which is followed by a formal hearing to judge the case. An example of this procedure can be seen among the Tiv people of northern Nigeria. A man who has a grievance waits until nightfall, when everything is quiet. Then he begins a loud song, accompanied by drumming, which explains what has happened and who is to blame. Sometimes his relatives may join in the song, giving their impressions of the case to make sure that the whole community hears all the details loud and clear.

The opponent then strikes up with a song of his own, putting his side of the case. This may go on for several nights, with the rivals

SINGING CONTEST
The singing contest is a traditional way of resolving disputes among the Inuit people of Greenland.

singing in their own compounds, and no one else getting a wink of sleep. When the rivals have run out of abuse, they may hire professional singers to carry on the good work. In earlier times, as the singing and dancing in the rival camps reached a crescendo, a fight would break out between the opponents, and the whole demonstration would turn into a brawl. Whichever rival won the fight also won the argument.

Nowadays, however, the dispute is not allowed to get to that stage. When the singing reaches a climax or looks as though it might develop into a brawl, the local leader calls the opponents to his compound and listens to them both singing and dancing.

The opponents are each allowed to present their side of the case to the leader who then makes a formal decision about who is right. Although the leader listens to the singing, it is not the songs which win the case. The person with the best songs can easily lose because the leader judges the case on the facts that are put before him.

The Tangue people of the north coast of New Guinea also use music, but not in a competitive way. There, music is purely a way of letting off steam and expressing anger or grievance at a situation. The angry, rapid drumbeats on a slit-gong will often bring the local men together to hear what the drummers have to say. The people with grievances make speeches in a gathering known as 'br'ngun'guni', in which eating plays an important part.

The crimes people are complaining about are often to do with the theft of food or resources, so the offering of food at a formal gathering helps to take the sting out of the situation and restore calm. In this case, the gathering is not aiming to make a judgement against one or other of the opponents but, rather like the singing of the Inuit, to allow each side to get rid of their anger and work towards agreement.

EXPRESSING GRIEVANCES
From Nigeria to New Guinea, people air their grievances with singing and drumming. In West Africa, drums are used for sending messages, so a complaint could be widely known very quickly.

Paying the Price

In some cases, the punishment for a crime is a prison sentence or a public humiliation of some kind. Sometimes it is death. But in other cases, the person has to pay some form of compensation to the aggrieved parties, rather like paying a fine of money for certain crimes in Western courts.

The earliest known example of people being charged monetary fines is the set of laws drawn up by King Ur-Nammu, ruler of Sumeria in about 2050 BC. According to these laws, a person who chopped off someone's foot could expect to pay ten silver shekels. Breaking a bone was not so serious and the fine was only one shekel.

In societies where the gods and spirits are involved in judgements, making lavish offerings to them is often the way of paying the price for crimes committed. Sometimes the person who has done wrong is thought to be possessed by an evil spirit. The Muslim Somali people explain many ills in this way, for example. The problem is resolved by making lavish offerings in an attempt to appease the evil spirit and persuade it to leave the person.

The Zande people of the Sudan have a strong tradition of witchcraft and sorcery. In the past, disputes often arose because one person was supposed to have practised witchcraft on someone else. For example, if someone was attacked by an animal while out hunting, that person could have been singled out by an enemy who had practised witchcraft to make the animal attack him.

The chief was called in to find out whether witchcraft had been used and if so,

WHEN SOMEONE SEEMS *to be possessed, offerings of jewellery or perfume are sometimes made to appease the spirits who might have attacked the victim.*

by whom. The chief would begin by questioning the person making the complaint, and use his knowledge of local affairs and gossip to make a decision. If this failed, a ritual procedure would be carried out. The person making the complaint would poison a chicken with a substance called 'benge'. He would then say who he thought had practised witchcraft on him and declaim the phrase, 'Oracle, if such is the case, kill the chicken.' If the chicken died, this proved that the accused person was guilty.

The person making the complaint would then go to the chief's court, and the chief would make a similar test with his own chicken. If this chicken died as well, no one could argue with the verdict. The person responsible for the witchcraft would be sent for and told to stop the evil influence.

Some societies use a mixture of formal trial proceedings and a more informal system. One example of this is the 'moot' of the Kpelle people of central Liberia. There are formal courts in Liberia, but for some cases, such as matrimonial differences, the Kpelle prefer to take their case to a moot which is a less formal meeting.

The meeting is called by the person making the complaint. This person chooses a relative who is also a town chief or elder to act as mediator or judge. The hearing is held in the complainant's home, but other people from the community squeeze in as well to hear what is going on. The complainant makes a speech, after which everyone present can ask questions. The accused then speaks and is questioned. Witnesses can also be called to speak and answer questions.

When all the evidence has been heard, the mediator sums up and gives an opinion on who is to blame, based on what everyone thinks. The person who is to blame then apologizes to the other person and presents small gifts, such as coins or clothing. The wronged person is also expected to give a small gift, usually a coin, to the guilty person. The guilty person has to pay the mediator and others who have heard the case by providing them with rum or beer to drink.

THE PEOPLE OF *Yap in the Pacific use stone discs to pay their debts and fines for disputes.*

National Disputes

The largest type of conflict or dispute is war. War involves many people and much bloodshed, and in the past, was often fought until one side was so severely crushed that the other could not help but emerge as victor. Today, a complex set of rules and rituals have been developed to bring about peace, either before a war can begin or in order to put an end to the fighting.

The procedure for settling a large conflict may not be so very different from the rituals used in individual disputes. A war between the followers of local tribes in a chiefdom such as Polynesia, in the Pacific Ocean, may be resolved by asking the chief to settle the dispute. In the same way, the Security Council of the United Nations can try to resolve larger-scale international conflicts.

Making peace is a matter of great importance where a foot wrong could alter the whole situation. Tribes or nations feel the need for some form of ritual to ensure that things will run smoothly. Sometimes, the supernatural is called in to help. In Borneo, for example, it was the custom for each of the warring parties to swear an oath of peace. As they made this oath, each of them would kill a pig. They thought that the gods might not be able to hear the oath for themselves, and that the animal's spirit would tell them that it had been sworn.

Modern peace talks normally take place around a table, with negotiators for both sides putting their case. Even a format which sounds as straightforward as this is surrounded by ritual. First, there will be 'negotiations about the negotiations', at which representatives from all parties discuss how the peace talks are to be conducted. Who will chair the talks? Who will the negotiators be? Where will the meeting be held, and what form will the discussion take?

Once the talks themselves start, more ritual comes into play. Everything has to be kept very secret, people behave in a diplomatic fashion even though they may be at odds with one another. Any disputes that do arise are glossed over to the general public reading newspapers or watching television. These procedures help the talks to run smoothly and prevent anyone losing face.

Protest Marches

People can make their feelings felt on matters of national concern, either as individuals in face-to-face disputes or

in large groups in demonstrations and protest marches. Demonstrators feel strongly about the subject they are protesting against and want to bring about change.

However, a demonstration is still a ritual procedure. People marching, shouting, carrying posters and banners: the whole scene is instantly recognizable to onlookers. The sheer numbers of people joining a protest group can be intimidating and threatening to outsiders. Today, with television crews and newspaper reporters on hand, demonstrators can make their point very forcibly to a large number of people.

In 1989, students in China began a mass demonstration against the country's regime. The students, who were campaigning for a more liberal and democratic government, began a mass hunger strike, and finally set up camp in Beijing's Tiananmen Square, where Chairman Mao had proclaimed the foundation of the People's Republic of China in 1949. The government's reaction was to send in the army. Tanks rumbled into the square, and there were days of killings and mass arrests. The demonstration and its aftermath was watched by most of the world, as television crews recorded the events.

MARCHING ON

The public demonstration is one of the most well-known ways of registering protest. One English protest march which has gone down in the history books is the Jarrow Hunger March which took place in 1936. Unemployed workers from the closed-down Jarrow shipyard in Tyne and Wear marched nearly 500 kilometres to London to protest about the unemployment and poverty that this closure had brought about. The march made its point forcibly and paved the way for the setting-up of new industries locally and elsewhere.

THE ART OF PROTEST

Protesters usually carry banners or placards, and some of these symbols have become world-famous. Examples range from the decorated banners of the trade unions and women's suffrage campaigners to symbols like those of anti-nuclear protesters and Poland's Solidarity movement.

Find Out Some More

BOOKS TO READ

Ancient Greece and Rome edited by Brian Williams (Cherrytree Press, 1992)

The Aztecs by Jacqueline Dineen (Heinemann Educational Books, 1992)

The Children's Encyclopedia (Dorling Kindersley, 1991)

Egypt and Mesopotamia by R.J. Unstead (A. & C. Black, 1985)

Food and Fasting by Deirdre Burke (Wayland, 1992)

The Greeks by Jacqueline Dineen Heinemann Educational Books, 1991)

The Greeks by Roy Burrell (Oxford University Press, 1990)

The Illustrated History of the World (Simon and Schuster Young Books, 1994)

Indiana Jones explores Ancient Egypt by John Malam (Evans, 1991)

Jewish Festivals by Jane Cooper (Wayland, 1989)

Religious Food by Jon Mayled and Aviva Paraiso (Wayland, 1987)

Timelines of the Ancient World by Chris Scarre (Dorling Kindersley, 1993)

The Vikings by Hazel Mary Martell (Heinemann Educational Books, 1991)

FOR OLDER READERS

You might like to try some of these books to find out more background information about some of the peoples in this book.

The Atlas of the Ancient World by Margaret Oliphant (Marshall Editions, 1992)

The Atlas of Early Man by Jacquetta Hawkes (Macmillan, 1976)

The Golden Bough (A History of Myth and Religion) by Sir James Frazer (Chancellor Press, 1994)

The Illustrated Guide to Classical Mythology by A.R. Hope Moncrieff (Studio Editions, 1992)

Kingdoms of Gold, Kingdoms of Jade (The Americas before Columbus) by Brian M. Fagan (Thames and Hudson, 1991)

Viking Age England by Julian D. Richards (Batsford, 1991)

World Mythology, general editor Roy Willis (Duncan Baird Publishers, 1993)

PLACES TO VISIT

Many museums have exhibits from the ancient world and events in history. Find out if there is a museum in your area which shows early people and farming methods.

- The British Museum has galleries on Greek, Roman, Egyptian, Western Asiatic, Oriental, Japanese and Medieval periods. Its address is: Great Russell Street, London WC1B 3DG. Telephone: 0171–636 1555.

- The Museum of Mankind displays artefacts from traditional cultures around the world. Its address is 6 Burlington Gardens, London W1X 2EX. Telephone: 0171–437 2224.

- The Victoria & Albert Museum has galleries devoted to China, Japan, India and Islam. Its address is: Cromwell Road, London SW7 2RL. Telephone: 0171–938 8500.

- The Jorvik Viking Centre, Coppergate, York (Telephone: 01904–643211) and the Manx Museum, Douglas, Isle of Man (Telephone: 01624–675522) both have excellent displays on the Vikings.

- To find out about beer festivals in Germany, contact the German Tourist Office in London (Telephone: 0891–600100).

- For information about wine festivals in France, telephone the French Tourist Office on 0891–244123.

Index